The Trinity and Culture

American University Studies

Series VII
Theology and Religion

Vol. 34

PETER LANG
New York · Bern · Frankfurt am Main · Paris

Charles Sherrard MacKenzie

The Trinity and Culture

PETER LANG
New York · Bern · Frankfurt am Main · Paris

Library of Congress Cataloging-in-Publication Data

MacKenzie, Charles Sherrard
  The Trinity and culture.

  (American university studies. Series VII, Theology and religion ; vol. 34)
    Bibliography : p.
    1. Trinity. 2. Sociology, Christian. I. Title.
II. Series.
BT111.2.M2   1987   231′.044   87-4224
ISBN 0-8204-0492-6
ISSN 0740-0446

CIP-Kurztitelaufnahme der Deutschen Bibliothek

MacKenzie, Charles Sherrard:
The Trinity and culture / Charles Sherrard MacKenzie. – New York; Bern; Frankfurt am Main; Paris: Lang, 1987.
  (American University Studies: Ser. 7,
  Theology and Religion; Vol. 34)
  ISBN 0-8204-0492-6

NE: American University Studies / 07

© Peter Lang Publishing, Inc., New York 1987

All rights reserved.
Reprint or reproduction, even partially, in all forms such as microfilm, xerography, microfiche, microcard, offset strictly prohibited.

Printed by Weihert-Druck GmbH, Darmstadt, West Germany

Contents

Preface.. vii

Chapter 1. Western Culture and Beliefs 1

An analysis of the values underlying western culture from ancient days to the present including the Trinitarian values and ideals which unified the culture of the Middle Ages

Chapter 2. The Church's Struggle to Understand God... 31

The historical development of the church's understanding of God as Triune

Chapter 3. A Contemporary Vision of the Trinity....... 63

A contemporary exploration into the Triunity of God. This chapter explores the nature of the unity of God. It also suggests that a plurality in God is required by love and pain in God.

Chapter 4. Certainty About the Triune God 85

Is the doctrine of the Trinity credible when subjected to truth criteria?

Chapter 5. The Trinity and Culture 95

Various models for relating Trinitarian Christianity to culture are discussed. (i.e. Augustine, Calvin, Pascal, Heim, de Chardin, etc.) The Trinity is presented as the ultimate theological paradigm

Chapter 6. The Trinity and the World 117
  The relationship between the Triune God, the world, and its peoples is explored.

Epilogue and Beginning 139

Bibliography 147

Preface

The twentieth century has been characterized by unprecedented conflict and strife as well as by a deterioration of long established values. The object of faith for many has changed. Once faith focused on a transcendent deity and on unchanging values. Now it kaleidoscopically shifts from human beings to their mental constructs to nature. The focus of faith changes, sometimes abruptly and without warning, driven by historical events, new discoveries and the moods of the masses. Consequently, the values by which people live change, social behavior is modified, and society suffers from value vertigo.

In the midst of a fragmented, crisis-ridden society, a host of people yearn for constancy and for an abiding value system which can unify their perceptions of reality. Through the centuries of western history, a vision of the Triune God has offered culture a framework of constancy and unity. At times it has brought some degree of harmony to society. These chapters suggest that a renewed vision of the Triune God "in whom we live and move and have our being" could provide the cultures of earth the values, stability, constancy, and unity they urgently need.

Chapter One explores various world views which have inspired either unity or division in western culture. It probes the fragmentation of contemporary culture. It suggests a possibility for a new cultural unity in the future. It indicates that humanity's vision of God has influenced culture profoundly in the past.

The chapters that follow trace the development of the Trinitarian understanding of God from ancient days to the present. They echo Biblical writers whose understanding of the Triune God ushered in a new era in human history because it prompted the emergence of a new humanity with new values, motivations, and aspirations. They highlight individuals who attempted to relate the Triune God to the culture of their days. The Augustinian Trinitarian principle with its emphasis on the sublime unity of God is outlined since Augustine's vision paved the way for a new unity in society. Pascal's vision of the unity of all things is described as it arose from his vision of God. As society more and more fragmented in the modern period, Hegel endeavored to develop a unifying view of the Triune God. These and others had a vision of the Trinity which influenced, to greater or lesser degrees, their contemporaries and impacted the values of their cultures.

In our day, a powerful, new vision of the Triune God is needed, a vision grand enough to enable the Church to become a unifying, stabilizing force in a society which is on the verge of the abyss. In this volume, we make a modest proposal which points in the direction of a renewed vision of the Trinity.

The final chapter of this work seeks to apply a renewed understanding of the Triune God to peoples of other world religions. A denouement in the epilogue briefly suggests how the Church may apply Trinitarian principles to society.

In summary, this book is an exploratory effort to understand the relevance of the Triune God to the contemporary world. It raises questions and offers suggestions but contains few definitive answers. The author is aware of its limitations. Yet, he hopes that by opening up the subject, he may evoke further consideration, study, and understanding of the relation between the Creator and His creation, between the Triune God and culture.

Two persons have assisted me with this project. My wife LaVonne MacKenzie provided inspiration and encouragement. My Administrative Assistant Rosalie Vouga, by her patient endurance, enabled me to put the manuscript in its present form. Any good which may result from this book is in part, due to their efforts. This volume's limitations, however, are the result of my own limitations.

The author shares the sentiment of John Newton:

> "Weak is the effort of my heart,
> And cold my warmest thought
> But when I see thee as thou art,
> I'll praise thee as I ought."

Charles S. MacKenzie, President
Grove City College, 1986

1

Western Culture and Beliefs

The quest for some unity underlying reality is as old as man himself. Many thoughtful people, rifted by the alienation of their higher from their lower selves, have sought some unity to overcome both the personal and the social alienations of life. In the midst of a fractured and fragmented world, many also have struggled to understand how the facets of existence relate to some whole. Age after age, people have sought unifying meaning amidst the fragments of experience. They have endeavored to weave pieces of knowledge together into some coherent pattern of meaning. Whenever numbers of people have achieved a consensus or some understanding of reality which provides them with answers to the "fundamental questions" of their lives,[1] they have drawn from it values which have guided them in building their societies and cultures. Each culture has reflected the questions, values, motifs, and patterns of meaning adopted by its people.

People have sought for answers to their fundamental questions in several directions. They have pursued a principle of meaning and unity in some transcendent realm overarching all things, or in the natural, physical world, or in their own inner experience, or in some combination of these.

Each culture has been shaped by a system of values which has emerged from the human quest for meaning and coherence. Many of the early Greeks derived meaning and values from a transcendent realm which they believed affected their lives. Later as men began to turn to the natural order seeking meaning in life, a shift occurred. The Graeco-Roman period was a transitional time when transcendent values existed in tension with values drawn from the natural order. Then material values came to dominance in ancient Rome. Another gigantic shift in values occurred when Rome's sensual and material values gave way to values stemming from the transcendent, Triune God worshipped by Christians. Christian values, communicated to society by the Catholic Church, dominated the culture of the Middle Ages (400 A.D.–1100 A.D.). Then came another transitional period when Christian values and the earthbound values of the Renaissance struggled with each other for dominance. With the dawning of the modern era (15th century to the present), another foundational shift in cultural values occurred. Values derived from nature came into ascendancy. Across the centuries, massive changes in values have produced gigantic changes in culture.

Major shifts in the values which undergird culture have not eliminated conflicting values. Transcendent, spiritual values have coexisted with material, sensual values in every culture. The changes in values which have occurred from time to time among masses of people in Western culture are described here in summary form. That does not suggest, however, that values which conflicted with the values of the majority were obliterated or eliminated. To the contrary, in every society, different value systems have existed side by side though one or another may have been most influential and most widely accepted.

It also must be recognized that while values have shaped cultures, cultures have influenced people's questions, answers, and values. Although people can be influenced and conditioned by the values of the cultures in which they live, people also create and change culture. People change their cultures partially in response to new questions posed by circumstances and to new answers and new values which inspire and motivate them. Values held by people can be affected by different values held by other people. People's values also can be affected by historical circumstance and geography. A culture may change as masses of people adopt a new value orientation in response either to the values held by others or to historical situations or to changes in geography or climate.

Although culture and personal values may interact and feed upon each other, personal values are the foundation of culture. If it were possible to withdraw personal values from people, culture would vanish. On the other hand if culture were destroyed, the people who would survive would create another culture to express the values they hold.

A survey of the shifting value systems in western culture begins in ancient Greece. The ancient Hellenes generally believed their existence was unified by an overarching, transcendent realm. The Myceneans (1599 B.C.–1100 B.C.) under a series of great kings such as Agamemnon worshipped a pantheon of gods creating traditions which ripened to give the Hellenes a cultural cohesion which became the basis for the later Homeric poems. Later, Hesiod in his *Theogony* told the story of the Olympian gods. Out of the void and darkness of chaos had come a male deity Uranus representing the heavens and a female deity Gaea representing the earth. They bore the Titans one of whom was Kronas who with his sister Rhea bore the Olympian deities (Zeus, Demeter, Hera, Pluto, Poseidon, Vesta). Zeus with his sister Hera, in turn, bore Apollo, Athena, Aphrodite, Artemis and others. This confusing array of deities had great power over mortals, yet their morality was like that of mortals. Zeus, for example, persisted in pursuing and seducing mortal girls. The gods were superior in power but not in morality. They used their power to intervene in human affairs whenever man, out of pride, dared to intrude into the domain of the gods. The Olympian gods, who drank and loved with passion, shared the moral weaknesses of men, so they did not judge men on the basis of morality. Rather, they punished and rewarded humans on the basis of personal disloyalty or for personal offences against the deity. Man was a creature at the mercy and the whim of the gods. Zeus condemned Ixion to eternal suffering for assaulting Hera, Zeus' wife. Sisyphos was punished for telling the secret of one of Zeus' intrigues. Prometheus' great sin was his effort to place in the hands of men powers which belonged to the gods. The gods had power. Men were creatures. Each was destined to live within his own order, to acknowledge his own limitations.

The Olympian gods, along with men, were subject to an even higher power, moira or destiny. Moira assigned to the gods and to men a destiny, a role in life. Although Achilles resorted to all manner of trickery in an effort to outwit his fate, he failed. The gods were limited by an overarching destiny (Moira). Herodotus remarked, "It is impossible even for a God to avoid the fate that is ordained." Destiny was essentially impersonal and amoral. A blind, automatic destiny wrought vengeance on those who challenged her decrees. Each man, each god had his own destined sphere within which he was free to act. His place was appointed to him by a powerful, but purposeless, destiny. Since destiny appointed the bounds of men and of gods, it was considered immoral for one to challenge destiny. Hubris, pride which challenges destiny, was the epitome of immorality and brought forth vengeance and retribution. Moira, because of its limiting power, generally has been understood as a negative force although its negative aspect may be the recoil of a positive, dynamic impulse toward order. Later Sophocles in *Oedipus Rex* would attempt to deal more fully with the question of fate.

In the late 9th or early 8th century, Homer in *The Iliad* and *The Odyssey* committed the ancient legends to writing. They became a guiding force in perpetuating the myths of higher powers which ruled human affairs. The gods of Olympus interacted with men. In *The Iliad* we read such things as "So he prayed, and Phoebus Apollo heard him. He came down from the summits of Olympus . . ." Again we read "it is Zeus who sends dreams . . ." "Perhaps in return for the smoke of lambs and sacrificial goats, he will save us from the pestilence . . ." "By the secret knowledge that Phoebus Apollo had given him he had guided the Achaean ships to Ilion." Men sought the gods for favors which they could grant in exchange for devotion. Yet destiny had fixed an impassable gulf between men and the gods. The ancient Greeks lived and died with a consciousness of Olympian heroes and of destiny which overarched their lives with aloof but ever-present power.

Then a shift occurred. Certain Greek thinkers began to explore nature in their quest for a basic unity underlying reality.

Thales of Miletus concluded that the many parts of physical reality resemble each other and are related to each other as forms of one basic element which was water. Thales' pupil Anaximander addressed himself to how the primary element could become many different things. Motion, which is eternal, separates off the elements from that boundless realm which he considered to be the primary stuff. Anaximenes, a young colleague of Anaximander, reasoned that the basic element was air. Quantitative changes in air (rarefaction and/or condensation) produce qualitative changes which account for all things. Heraclitus continued the search for a basic unity amidst a changing world. He concluded that "all things are in flux" and that the basic element which changes is FIRE which he called God. God is the universal reason immanent in all things including man. Eternal fire follows the direction of universal reason (Logos) which is one with it. It changes its form, but nothing ever is lost. Parmenides of Elea, while rejecting the idea of change, calling it a confusion of appearances with reality, described the basic substance as eternal Being which is permanent and unchanging. Empedocles of Sicily attempted a reconciliation of the various points of view. He stated that Parmenides was correct in saying that the basic stuff of reality was eternal and unchanging, but he said there is not one basic element but four—earth, air, fire, and water. Pythagoras in his search for the basic, universal stuff of reality abandoned the idea that it could be found through the senses. He adopted the notion that there was a non-material, mathematical pattern of forms existing in a transcendent realm. It has no material substance but shapes all of reality. He laid the foundation for Plato's teaching about eternal Ideas.

Some Greeks had glimpsed a unifying force in the transcendence of moira and the power of the Olympian gods, others sought that unity by exploring nature, and still others sought that unity in a more inward, mental direction. Socrates urged his followers to seek the truth within themselves. He developed the notion of the soul, man's psyche. The soul was man's conscious, structured personality, an inner capacity for intelligence and morality. The soul was the seat of knowing, which directs man's behavior toward virtue.

With Plato, Greek thought reached its apogee. His great mind encompassed the thoughts of the Milesians, the Eleatics, Heraclitus, the Pythagoreans and his teacher Socrates. He blended their best insights into one comprehensive philosophy which has influenced Western culture to this day.

He described the world of material things in motion as the realm of shadowy appearances or becoming. Above and beyond this transitory, material world of becoming and flux is the transcendent world of eternal Ideas or Being. The material world of becoming is dependent upon and participates in the overarching realm of Ideas which is ultimately real. The world of Ideas is eternal and unchanging. It explains all existence because it is the invisible realm of pure essences. It provides stability, constancy and unity to all reality because it is unchanging. It is approached by man as he turns inward and climbs toward the Ideas through rational contemplation and thought. Plato thus pointed the Greeks and Western culture toward invisible, eternal, unchanging Ideas in a transcendent realm beyond sense and matter. In that realm was to be found the unity, meaning, and purpose which unified all of reality. This transcendent, unifying force described by Plato directed much of Greek thought and has influenced profoundly all of western culture.

But in the centuries that followed a massive shift occurred. In the minds of many leaders in Graeco-Roman society, the transcendent Ideas of Plato were replaced by an emphasis on the physical and material forces of life. The shift began with Aristotle's description of reality. Instead of seeing the Ideas or Forms existing in a transcendent realm, Aristotle saw them existing in the things of the material world. For example, the idea or form of treeness existed in each tree. This emphasis brought renewed attention to the material order. The world of becoming became nearly as significant as the world of Being (Forms/Ideas).

Epicurus and the Epicureans went even further by picturing the world as consisting of eternal atoms which were tiny, indestructible bits of matter. For Epicurus, only matter existed. There was no god. Even human nature was composed of atoms which constituted human thoughts and feelings. The Epicureans emphasized pleasure as the goal of life. The ultimate pleasure was peace of mind and absence of bodily pain.

The Stoics continued the emphasis on materiality. For them matter was the ultimately real. In addition to inert matter there was a form of matter which was constantly in motion and which was rational. It was material fire which had the attribute of rationality and which, for the Stoics, was understood to be god. God was the fire, force, logos, reason which underlies structures and orders passive, inert matter. In that sense, god was both a material substance and the soul of the universe. Man contained a spark of divinity because man contained part of the substance of god. This fiery, material, rational substance unified all reality.

During much of the Graeco-Roman period the unity of reality was understood to lie in nature and the material realm. Greek thought, morals and art were carried to Rome by a host of Graeculi or "Greeklings" as they were called. They became tutors, teachers and lecturers to many of the Roman upper class and spread Greek thought throughout Rome. Followers of Epicurus paved the way for the Roman Lucretius who taught that nature was self-contained and autonomous. He called religion the prime evil in society and declared that nothing exists but atoms and the void. Graeculi of Stoic persuasion penetrated the Roman intellectual class so that Cato the younger, Epictetus, Scipio, Cicero, Seneca, Trajan, and Marcus Aurelius were influenced by Stoic ideals. Indeed, for a time Stoicism was called the conscience of Rome.

Roman society centered itself increasingly on material values. Some of Rome's great monuments such as the Pantheon, the Coliseum, the aqueducts and the arches erected to commemorate the achievements and victories of its leaders illustrate the materiality of Roman culture. The awe-inspiring Pantheon, which was the shrine of seven planetary deities, had a massiveness and solidity which suggests mass turning back on itself. The Coliseum, (80 A.D.) used for sports extravaganzas, symbolized material pleasures linked to functionality as it wove together conflicting forms (open arches and solid walls) in splendid harmony. The Roman aqueducts displayed a pragmatic, utilitarian quest for comfort and convenience linked to practical engineering skills. The monumental arches, celebrating Roman victories, were monuments to raw, brute, material power.

Roman sculpture and art also expressed the material values at the heart of Roman culture. For example, the impressive statue of Augustus of Primaporta (c. 20 B.C.) by its effective tactile depiction of consular costume gives a sensory impression of immediacy. Augustus' right arm, raised in commanding gesture, bespeaks physical power. Another example may be found in the painting of "Hercules Discovering the Infant Telephus in Arcadia." This was found in the Basilica of Herculaneum which was destroyed in the eruption of Vesuvius in 79 A.D. Hercules is portrayed as a man of great physical power with strong muscles and imposing build. The work is three dimensional and yields powerful sense impressions. The culture that was Rome was moving more and more toward the exaltation of the sensory and the sensual.

The ancient Roman deities increasingly became objects of ridicule. Martial and Juvenal openly scoffed at them. Yet Roman leaders, largely for political reasons, tried to resurrect faith in the ancient gods. At the same time, new deities were being brought to Rome. The Egyptian Isis, the Syrian Atargatis, the Parthian Mithra, the Jewish Yahweh won followers amongst the common people of Rome who yearned for mystical experiences and for promises of immortality. Yet most Romans eventually succumbed to spiritual and cultural disillusionment. The gods seemed impotent. Philosophy was above the common man. Lucretius was too sophisticated to reach the masses. Eventually even Stoicism, which for 400 years penetrated the upper classes, lost its appeal. Rome became more and more sensual, brutal and preoccupied with the practical affairs of the material world.

At the same time, new spiritual forces appeared on the horizon. The Jewish Philo of Alexandria was steeped in both Jewish and Greek thought which he attempted to synthesize. His concept of the Logos profoundly influenced many. What the Stoics called the Logos or reason shaping all things received a new description by Philo. Drawing on his knowledge of the wisdom literature of the Old Testament, he depicted the Logos as a person and stated that God revealed Himself through the Logos. God for Philo was eternal, spiritual and the essential soul of the universe. He was distinct from created matter though matter had no motion or life unless it was infused by the Logos and its instrumentalities (i.e. Plato's Ideas, Jewish angels, etc.). Philo deeply influenced the development of emerging Christian, Gnostic, and Neo-Platonic doctrines. He helped to pave the way for the new, Christian vision of reality which later would displace many of the old, sensual, materialistic perspectives of the Graeco-Roman world.

With the spread of the Christian gospel around the Mediterranean, a radically new vision of transcendence was presented to the world. The God of the Christians was proclaimed as eternal, unchanging, personal, loving, completely transcendent yet thoroughly immanent. God was revealed to be a holy, loving Father who had become incarnate in the carpenter from Nazareth, Jesus Christ. Jesus Christ had lived the exemplary life, had died bearing the sins of humanity and had risen bodily from the dead. The promises of forgiveness, of eternal life and of a new and a personal relationship with the Infinite God were extended to all mankind.

Carried by fervent believers, the Christian message spread rapidly throughout and beyond the Empire. It was appealing to an empire of 40 million slaves and unnumbered millions shackled by poverty because it proclaimed God's love for all, liberation of the human spirit, equality before God, compassion instead of hatred, forgiveness for the guilt laden and endless happiness beyond the grave to those who daily faced death. By the year 300 A.D. Smyrna and Ephesus were predominantly Christian, and Rome numbered about 100,000 as Christians. By that time perhaps as many as 20% of the Empire considered themselves to be Christians. No wonder Tertullian declared "Already we fill the world."

This was a religion of the spirit which pointed humanity toward a God of holiness and love. It proclaimed that the transcendent God had come to dwell in and among His people. It called the followers of the Christ to holy living and to the simple life. It shunned the appetites of the flesh and insisted that those with this world's goods must share them with their poorer brethren. It was in sharp contrast to the sensuality and materialism which had inundated the Empire.

Yet Christianity was not the only force which emerged to point people toward the spiritual. NeoPythagoreans and Neoplatonists also were proclaiming the reality of supersensible realities by reviving Pythagoras' teaching on the transmigration of the soul and Plato's doctrine of transcendent Ideas.

Plotinus (204–270 A.D.) forcefully expressed such mystical and spiritual aspirations. He wedded philosophic speculation to a religious plan of salvation. A student of Ammonius Saccas, he was impressed with his teacher's efforts to reconcile Christianity with Plato. Plotinus acknowledged the existence of matter but believed that matter was not the ultimate reality. The true reality is God who can be reached only by mystical ecstasy. God is the One eternal, unchanging, undefinable, indivisible, unifying absolute. All things emanate from God. The first and highest emanation from God was Mind. It is like the One though it is not absolute. Each succeeding emanation brings into being a subordinate emanation. Mind begets the World Soul which begets the human soul which begets matter. Each emanation overflows into the one it begets. Matter is the dimmest emanation which is farthest from the One who is absolute reality. It approaches the boundary of utter nothingness. Matter or body is evil since it is at the outer fringe, farthest away from God and rationality.

Plotinus held that the soul's ascent to unity with the One is painful and difficult. The material world must be renounced as one painfully climbs the ladder of knowledge toward union with God in a mystic rapture where there is no longer consciousness of the soul's separation from the Absolute. Proper behavior, correct thinking and the right use of the emotions can lead to ecstatic union with God who is the ultimate unity that brings all things into harmony.

The philosophy of Plotinus was preserved by his pupil Porphyry who assembled 54 treatises of Plotinus into six sets of nine called the *Enneads*. Although Plotinus' views were too complicated to appeal to the masses, his Neoplatonism touched the upper class intellectuals including the Emperor Gallienus and Augustine. His invitation to undertake a pilgrimage toward unity with the Absolute above and beyond all things would be heeded by Pseudo-Dionysius (c. 500 A.D.) and many others during the next thousand years.

The Emperor Constantine, however, ushered in a new age based on transcendent values when he aligned the Roman Empire with Christianity. Instead of the materialistic, Graeco-Roman values of earlier centuries, transcendent, spiritual values became the basis of society for the next one thousand years.

This was a major turning point in the history of Western culture. Meaning and the unification of society would be sought not in earthbound, sensate philosophies, but in spiritual and transcendent perspectives.

It often has been pointed out that Constantine probably took this step more for political than spiritual reasons. The Roman Empire had fallen into serious disrepair. Morality was at a low ebb. Family life was disintegrating as divorce, homosexuality and licentiousness became widespread. War on many different frontiers had drained the resources of the empire. Inflation had skyrocketed, bankruptcies had increased and for a while a state socialism had been tried. Class hatred had reached a fever pitch. Constantine hoped that Christianity would give the empire new moral muscle, a revival of family life, prosperity, a new era of peace and above all a new vision of unity which would rally support for the imperial throne.

But the emperor found that two bitter disputes were dividing the Christian church: the Donatist controversy and the Arian heresy. The Donatists were refusing to recognize bishops who had compromised the faith during the years of persecution. Constantine, in quest of unity, called a council of bishops at

Arles (314) which denounced the Donatists and ordered them to return to the Catholic church. Although the Donatist controversy would continue to simmer in the life of the church for years to come, Constantine sought to unify a divided church.

Next Constantine sought a resolution to the Arian debates in the church. About 318, Arius, a tall, thin, melancholy priest in Egypt declared that Christ was not completely one with the Creator God, but that he was the foremost and the highest of all created beings. Christ was not coeternal with the Father. The Holy Spirit, in turn, was begotten from Christ and was less than truly God. The Neoplatonic influence upon Arius had been significant.

When Arius' bishop Alexander persuaded a council of Egyptian bishops to defrock Arius, division spread quickly throughout the Eastern church. Constantine, who had hoped that the Church would become a unifying force for the empire, wrote to Arius and Alexander chiding them both. His letter discloses his longing for unity.

> "I had proposed to lead back to a single form the ideas which all people conceive of the Deity; for I feel strongly that if I could induce men to unite on that subject, the conduct of public affairs would be considerably eased."[2]

Nevertheless, Constantine's appeal was of no effect. The debate raged throughout the Eastern church. Many felt that the whole fabric of Christian belief would unravel if Christ was not acknowledged as truly God. So the controversy spread.

Constantine was determined to end the strife. He issued a call for the first universal council of the church to meet in Nicaea in 325. Three hundred eighteen bishops, mostly from the Eastern provinces, gathered along with a host of lower clerics at Nicaea in Bithynia. Arius reaffirmed his view that Christ was created and was not equal to the Father. Athanasius, Bishop Alexander's young but brilliant Archdeacon, declared that if Christ and the Holy Spirit were not of one substance with the Father, polytheism would result. Only a handful of bishops, along with Arius, refused to sign the creed which the council finally issued. It read:

"We believe in one God, the Father Almighty maker of all things visible and invisible; and in one Lord Jesus Christ, the Son of God begotten . . . not made, being of one essence (homoousion) with the Father . . ."

With that the council of Nicaea was ended. It was the beginning, however, of an explicit consensus about the central belief of Christianity. It gave the church a basic doctrine to which, in future centuries, most Christians scattered across the world would subscribe. A new era with new values was under way.

For nearly a thousand years, western culture was permeated with values derived from this Trinitarian faith. These values unified and integrated society to a remarkable degree. The Catholic church as the teacher of Christian doctrines and values was the visible expression of that unity. As a patron of the arts and of letters, it shaped Christian culture. As the primary sponsor of what religious education was available, it channeled its values to generation after generation of young people. As the guardian of morality for the social order, it left its mark on the law of Western nations.

At the core of Christian teaching was the doctrine of the Trinity. Although the council of Nicaea summarized the church's belief in the Holy Trinity, Augustine and other theological minds explicated that belief more fully. The council of the church at Chalcedon (451) clarified more fully the nature of Jesus Christ.

It was Augustine who related the unity of the Triune God to society in such a way that the Trinitarian principle became a unifying force for western society during the Middle Ages. That vision of the Trinity not only unified but also humanized and sacralized society for centuries to come.

Augustine's emphasis on the Trinity inspired churchmen during the Middle Ages to focus upon the transcendent realm as the source of their values. The empirical and the secular faded. The church, Trinitarian in doctrine, controlled politics, education, and culture in general. Boethius (480–524), Pseudo-Dionysius (c. 500), John Scotus Erigena (b. 810), Peter Abelard (1079–1142), and others who endeavored to interpret Plato and

Aristotle in light of Trinitarian faith also helped to keep culture focused on transcendent values.

Transcendent Christian values were reflected in much of the literature, drama and music of the Middle Ages. Morality plays such as *Everyman* played in just about every church and village of Europe. It stressed that man's ultimate destiny lies beyond the grave. Dante (1265–1321) in his *Divine Comedy* also emphasized that man's ultimate purpose was the attainment of heaven. He also dignified man by acknowledging his free will. Nevertheless, union with God was man's goal. Literature and music generally were facets of the great cultural unity which centered on God. After Pope Gregory I (540–604), the monophonic Gregorian chant inspired feelings of sublime reverence in churches across the Empire. As the Middle Ages waned, however, the impious Goliards (10th-13th centuries) popularized love songs and drinking songs. The jongleurs in France entertained and sang in a worldly vein and troubadours began to sing of chivalric ideals.

Perhaps the most visible expression of the spiritual values which unified the Middle Ages were the great churches and cathedrals. Hagia Sophia ("Church of Holy Wisdom") in Constantinople, consecrated in 537, was an architectural triumph. Its great dome, resting upon a ring of forty windows, seems to float over a gigantic nave. Hagia Sophia along with other Byzantine churches were spiritual visions captured in brick and mortar.

In the West the late Middle Ages saw a flowering of man's spiritual aspirations. In the eleventh century there was a great burst of church construction until just about every village had its own church. Many were beautifully adorned with windows and sculptures which celebrated man's spiritual convictions. Great Gothic cathedrals, most dedicated to the Virgin Mary, began to rise in the twelfth century. Two of the best known are Notre Dame of Paris, which was built between 1163 and 1200 and Chartres Cathedral, which took shape between 1194 and 1260. These great cathedrals emerged along with the rise and growth of the great cities of Europe. Most cathedrals served both religious and secular purposes. (i.e. worship, theater, lectures, court and general meetings of the citizenry). Yet both church and community felt at home amidst soaring stones reaching up toward infinity. These cathedrals were Bibles in stone. They reflected the unity of thought and the unified aspirations of the times.

For nearly five hundred years culture was almost exclusively dominated by Judeo-Christian values. There were almost no outstanding secular contributions to art or literature. But in the late middle ages that vision of unity began to unravel. The growth of cities, trade and wealth contributed greatly to the secularization of Europe. The unity of western culture began to fracture. A vision of the Trinity who unites all things began to fade as material, worldly concerns began to revive and to overshadow the cultural landscape with the approach of the Renaissance.

Part of the groundwork for a new humanism was laid by the dualism of Thomas Aquinas (1225–1274). Like his teacher Albert the Great, Aquinas struggled to define the boundaries between faith and reason, between theology and philosophy. Like Aristotle, he held that philosophy begins with a study of the objects of sense experience and reasons upward to the first cause, which is God. Man, he said, is capable of reasoning from the material world to first principles without assistance from divine revelation. This admission was a step in the direction of declaring man's intellectual autonomy and independence from God.

On the other hand, Thomas, in discussing theology, acknowledged the significance of God and revelation. Theology dealt with what man needs to know for salvation. Some truths he declared can be known only by revelation (i.e. that God is Triune). Philosophy discovers that God exists, but theology is necessary to declare His essence and nature. So Thomas distinguished between the spiritual realm where revelation is necessary and the realm of nature where man is capable of discovering truth without recourse to God's revelation. The practical effect was that this gave the green light to autonomous man to explore the realm of nature independent of God.

As a new age began to dawn, the classical writers of ancient Greece and Rome were being rediscovered. Greek manuscripts were being widely read and circulated. The Renaissance became a time of new, earth-centered discoveries. This can be seen by the progressive exaltation of nature in art and literature. Giotto, Masaccio, and Petrarch in their works became part of the movement toward emphasizing nature. Masaccio (1401–1428) was the first Renaissance artist who disregarded metaphysics and used illusion to describe the world. He used Christian subject matter, but painted in a secular fashion. His figures are real men who do not exhibit any noticeable spiritual characteristics. His work can be comprehended only by the senses because of its spatial, anatomical and psychological illusions. Petrarch (1304–1374) focused on the deep joys and sorrows of the natural man. Boccaccio (1313–1375) vividly described man's sensual appetites. Michelangelo (1475–1564), while still depicting religious themes, presented them with a strong, studied emphasis on the beauty of the physical body. Leonardo da Vinci (1452–1519) focused with exquisite care on the details of the human anatomy. Slowly man and nature were coming into new prominence. Pico della Mirandola (1463–1494) summed up the Renaissance mood as he pictured God declaring to man: "We have set thee at the world's center . . . as though the maker and molder of thyself, thou mayest fashion thyself in whatever shape thou shalt prefer . . ." This emphasis on man and nature would gradually replace God as the center of culture and eventually would dominate all of western culture.

Some of the seeds of modern technology, which later would become the focus of modern man's concern with nature and the world, also were beginning to germinate as man began to emerge from the otherworldly Middle Ages. For example, the Benedictine monks began to combine the theoretical and the practical in their daily life styles. Formerly, learned men did not work or get their hands dirty. That was left to slaves. The monk became the first intellectual "to get dirt under his fingernails" as he worked in the field or in the shop. The Benedictine message that "to labor is to pray" helped to introduce a new social atmosphere which would become more conducive to the development of technology. This, too, reflected a dawning appreciation of the goodness of the natural world. Man would come to find pleasure in his involvement with the world of nature.

Nature more and more began to be harnessed to work for human benefit. From the late tenth century onward water wheels came to be used to assist man. They were applied to an expanding number of industrial activities. About 1200 A.D., the windmill began to appear throughout Europe. Nature was becoming a source of power for man's technological advances. Man's appetite to harness the power of nature for his own use was being whetted. That appetite would grow to mammoth proportions in the centuries ahead.

The disintegration of the medieval cultural unity was accelerated by Johann Gutenberg's invention of movable type (1545) making possible the wide dissemination of new ideas. The medieval unity also was shattered by the opening up of new worlds by Columbus, Prince Henry, Magellan, and Cabot. Cultural unity was broken by new developments in science. Nicholas Copernicus (1473–1543) advanced the view that the center of our solar system was the sun, not the earth. He pointed out that mathematical calculations were much more meaningful if the sun was accepted as the center of the universe. Tycho Brahe, Kepler, and Galileo confirmed the Copernican view in spite of strong opposition from the church. This new description of the solar system forced upon culture a whole new understanding of man's relation to the universe. No longer was man the center of the material cosmos. Man's identity was in question. In addition, the authority and reliability of the church, large segments of which persisted in saying that the earth was indeed the center of all things, was challenged.

The rise of the Reformation further accelerated the disintegration of Medieval unity. Martin Luther (1483–1546), John Calvin (1509–1564) and other reformers led large sections of Europe in a revolt against the authority and infallibility of the Roman Church. No longer was the grace of God understood to be mediated exclusively by one church. The individual was emphasized as the proper interpreter of Scripture. Individualism was affirmed. Capitalism, work, and the acquisition of material wealth were sanctioned as signs of God's blessing upon the faithful. Although the Protestant Reformation gave priority to the individual's relationship to a transcendent God, it also resulted in a fragmenting of society and a new focus on life in the world.

The rapid rise of capitalism spawned new production methods, an increase in material goods and the emergence of manufacturing to meet human needs and desires. It also gave ever-increasing prominence to cities where people were flocking to obtain jobs in factories which were proliferating.

A new age was dawning which would be vastly different from the Middle Ages. The unity of the religious world was shattered as the church sundered. Old perceptions of the cosmos were broken by the new science. The unity of a feudalistic economic order was fragmented by the emerging capitalism.

Sir Francis Bacon (1561–1626) sought "the total reconstruction of the sciences, arts and all human knowledge." He represented the wave of discontent with medieval thought as he sought a new method of acquiring knowledge. He emphasized particular objects, empirical observations, experimentation and the discovery of natural laws through induction. He underestimated the role of mathematics and assumed that if one studied enough particular facts, a hypothesis would eventually emerge. He missed the point that the scientist must begin with a hypothesis and then test it by experimentation. Nevertheless, Bacon broke the grip of medieval philosophy and took a giant step toward making thought scientific.

It was Rene Descartes (1596–1650), however, who laid the keystone for modern thought. His method was to base knowledge upon a starting point which, to his mind, had absolute certainty. He used methodical doubt to eliminate false notions. By doubting and questioning everything, he sought to arrive at an absolutely certain starting point for knowledge. Unlike thinkers of the medieval period, he wiped out the assumption or presupposition that God exists. In the Middle Ages, philosophers had done their thinking against the backdrop of belief in the existence of God. Not so with Descartes. He doubted everything until he arrived at what for him was certain. That starting point was "I think therefore I am" (cogito ergo sum).

The existence of the thinking self became the starting point for knowledge. This was a sharp break with the past, but it would be adopted by a host of other thinkers as the modern world unfolded. Using both the rational argument of causation and his own version of Anselm's ontological argument, Descartes then proceeded to demonstrate logically that God exists.

Once he had convinced himself that God exists, he proceeded to lay a foundation for knowledge of the physical world. He reasoned that God guarantees that sense impressions impinging upon man correspond to actual, physical objects. The notion of God assured Descartes that the physical world actually exists. Later Pascal would accuse Descartes of using God merely to guarantee the physical world's existence. Pascal's criticism has cogency, for Descartes was indeed preoccupied with thinking man and the physical world rather than God who had been eliminated both as the starting point and as the center of Descartes' philosophy. God really had no function to fulfill other than to bridge the gap between thinking man and the world.

In addition, Descartes in developing his philosophy made nature into a gigantic machine. Space and extension were the basic reality. Purpose and spiritual reality disappeared from nature. The direction of modern thought had shifted radically.

John Locke (1632–1704) continued the emphasis on nature and the empirical. He stated that ideas are generated by the physical objects we experience. Sensation precedes reflection. Each person's mind at birth is like a blank sheet of paper upon which sense impressions impact to form ideas. Simple and complex ideas can be related to each other depending either upon the objects from which they come or upon the inclination of the mind itself.

Locke also emphasized the natural and moral laws of God which can be known by reason. The natural law implied that man has certain natural rights, particularly the right to own private property. Locke concluded that "the state of nature" should guide men's actions and should be the basis for human society.

Sir Isaac Newton (1642–1727) made the foundations firm for a view which saw the universe as a gigantic machine functioning according to material law. Building upon Galileo's and Kepler's empirical observations, Newton saw certain laws operating in the movement of the planets around the sun. He saw one universal force, gravitation, governing all physical objects. This had startling repercussions. God was relegated to a position of merely monitoring the motions of bodies which functioned according to the laws He had created.

The prominence of nature in the modern world was given a major boost by Jean Jacques Rousseau (1712–1778), who extolled the "noble savages" whose nobility he traced to their living close to nature. Unlike rationalists such as Descartes and Locke, Rousseau argued that natural intuition is to be trusted more than reason. Rousseau inaugurated a Romantic movement which has been exceedingly powerful from his day to ours. It urged all men to conform to nature.

It was Immanuel Kant (1724–1804), however, who effectively dismissed God from philosophy so that men became free to exalt man or nature to the central place in modern life. Kant, like the empiricists, maintained that for man knowledge is impossible without experience and sense impressions. David Hume, who greatly influenced Kant, had insisted that all knowledge is derived from experience and that we cannot have knowledge of anything that is nonsensory. Kant inquired whether this applied to God.

He concluded that though all knowledge begins with sense experience, it does not necessarily arise out of experience. The human mind is so constituted that it takes the data of sensory impressions and arranges them into knowledge. The mind is an active manufacturer of knowledge. This was a revolution of Copernican proportions in human thought. The mind brings to the process of knowledge categories and intuitions which it applies to the data of experience Man and the human mind were moved into the center of the universe instead of God. Yet the phenomenal world as people experience it was real and necessary to achieve knowledge. Kant acknowledged that a noumenal, non-sensory reality, the thing-in-itself (Ding an sich) existed, but that we cannot know it because we cannot experience it through the senses.

Yet humanity relentlessly attempts to unify reality by calling into play ideas of the self, the cosmos and God. Kant had declared that these are transcendental, unknowable ideas because we cannot experience them as empirical objects. Yet the idea of God seems necessary both to unify things and to provide a ground for morality. So Kant *postulated* the idea of God. He was careful to point out that man can neither prove nor disprove God's existence. Consequently, all he could do was postulate the idea of God since it could not be experienced empirically. The idea of God had been reduced to a postulate tacked on to philosophy.

As western culture entered the 19th century, it was becoming more and more captive to sensory values. In 1765 James Watt produced the steam engine. In 1807 the steamship *Clermont* sailed up the Hudson River. Steam engines which could drive a myriad of machines and wheels opened up new continents and a new age of industrial expansion. New products appeared for the mass market. People's appetite for material goods was stimulated.

The 19th century also saw Charles Darwin present his theory of biological evolution. His *Origin of the Species* appeared in 1859. Although Goethe and others had proposed ideas of organic development, Darwin presented a comprehensive view of evolution. The implications of Darwin's views were far-reaching. The emphasis was on physical development without any recourse to vitalism or to any spiritual power. The processes of evolution as described by Darwin did not need God or spirit. The survival of the fittest was a driving force in the whole process. Man came to be seen as just part of nature and its processes.

In Europe, the world of art also reflected a progressive materialization of values. The Baroque art of Caraveggio (1573–1610), Rubens (1577–1640), Bernini (1592–1680) and others displayed a bold naturalism, a heavy emphasis on color and an appeal to the sensual. For example, Rubens' "The Assumption of the Virgin" depicts a sensual beauty surrounded by fleshy, infant angels. Rembrandt van Rijn (1606–1669) probed the human psyche and depicted questions which were troubling people of his time.

Literature also was discussing questions with which restless people were wrestling. John Wolfgang von Goethe, in the midst of the "storm and stress" movement of Romanticism, completed his final draft of *Faust* in 1832. Faust was the penultimate man absorbed entirely in his own individual desires. Faust, progressively abandoned all values. The individual, creating grand schemes to conquer the world, operates without transcendent values although he seeks to act in accord with the natural laws which govern a machine-like world.

The 19th century realist and impressionist movements, in their attempts to come to grips with reality, rejected the romantics' and neoclassicists' wild use of imagination as it exalted heroic man. Impressionists like Edouard Manet (1832–1883), Claude Monet (1840–1926), and Pierre Renoir (1841–1919) looked to nature and painted what they seemed to see. They incorporated the effects of light into their works. Manet particularly led the world of art toward non-objective portrayals of reality which raised the question whether or not there is any reality beyond man's sensations. Vincent van Gogh (1853–1890) used vivid colors and distorted lines, not to depict what was there, but to describe the inner feelings which objects aroused in him. Thus, the center of art shifted dramatically from the objective world to the inner life of man. Just as Kant effected a Copernican revolution by making the mind of man the center of knowledge, art was moving to make man's feelings the center of things.

Matisse (1869–1954), Rouault (1871–1958), Gauguin (1848–1903), Cezanne (1839–1906), and Picasso (1881–1973) continued to make art earthbound. They abandoned the classical tradition of spatial composition. They also rejected the impressionist style where light dissolved form creating a new unity. For example, Cezanne focused on forms such as cylinders, spheres and cones.

He rearranged forms to recreate nature in patterns of geometric harmony. The artist had become the creator of his own new universe. Cubism and expressionism continued the effort at recreating the world.

The 20th century saw an increasing exaltation of man and earthly values. The churches, which had previously pointed humanity toward transcendent values even in the midst of a progressive materialization of society's values, became increasingly earthbound. Reliance upon the authority and reliability of the Bible declined as the findings of higher criticism came to be accepted. Building on the work of Jean Astruc (1753) and Johann Eichorn (1752–1827) who had noted an alternating use of the words Elohim and Yahweh for God in the Old Testament, Herman Hupfield (1853), Karl Graf (1865), and Julius Wellhausen (1844–1918) developed the view that the first few books of the Bible were composed of several earlier documents which had been combined by some unknown redactor. This type of theorizing seemed to the ordinary layman to reduce the Bible to a human document similar to other great literature which had been compiled under the impact of cultural and natural forces. Critical theories about the Bible coupled with new contacts with other world religions seemed to put the Judeo-Christian Scriptures on a level with the sacred writings of other cultures and religions. Many clergy, influenced by such views, tended to reflect a lower view of Scripture to the public. Preaching for the salvation of souls came to be replaced by discussions of worldly concerns in numerous pulpits. As Herman Randall, Jr. put it, "The outstanding religious phenomenon of the century has been not so much the fading of faith, as its transfer from a theological and cosmic to a human and social object."[3]

At the same time, the theological views of liberal thinkers of the 18th and 19th centuries were seeping down into grass roots Christianity. Following Kant's example, Schleiermacher, Ritschl, and Herrmann shifted the basis of theological thought from the Biblical revelation of a transcendent deity to human experience. The experience of the divine in the human psyche became the source of theological statements.

The shift in theological focus toward man was reflected in the rise of the social gospel. At the beginning of the 20th century Walter Rauschenbusch defined Christianity as the "religion of Jesus" which was understood to be a call for changing the social order. Rauschenbusch stated "The Kingdom of God is a collective conception . . . it is not a matter of saving human atoms, but of saving the social organism . . . That was the faith of Jesus."[4] Rauschenbusch influenced generations of Protestant clergy.

Some in the "social gospel" movement appeared to be mildly socialistic. Sherwood Eddy, Harry Ward, and Reinbold Niebuhr became leaders in the effort to provide religious support for secular, social movements.

Although the efforts of fundamentalists as well as neo-orthodox theologians like Karl Barth and Emil Brunner to keep theology Biblically-based produced sparks of transcendence in the church, most 20th century denominations became increasingly secularized. Some denominations became heavily involved in protest movements for civil rights, women's rights, and homosexual rights. The peace movement became a major priority. Boycotts against corporations became frequent. Major denominations gave lip service to transcendent ideals, but their major activities focused on social objectives. Theology increasingly moved in an earthbound direction with the spread of Bultmannian notions of a demythologized Bible, with the emergence of "death of God" theologies and with the rise of liberation theologies which sought the destruction of old social structures. Liberal theologies and the churches which promulgated them became absorbed in the here and now thus contributing to the demise of transcendence in contemporary culture.

Meanwhile 20th century science sent a tidal wave of new values across culture. The historian Herbert Butterfield wrote that the philosophic implication of the scientific revolution "outshines everything since the rise of Christianity and reduces the Renaissance and Reformation to the rank of mere episodes, mere internal displacements within the system of medieval Christendom."[5] That revolution had its roots in earlier centuries when a heliocentric universe had been affirmed by Copernicus, when the scientific method stressing induction and experimentation had been established, and when the Darwinian notion of natural evolution had received widespread acceptance influencing social and political thought. Each of these significant discoveries had become deeply ingrained in 20th century thought and tended to shift culture's focus from transcendent, spiritual reality to nature.

Man's view of nature underwent a radical change in the 20th century. The Newtonian view of nature as analagous to a gigantic, mechanical machine was abandoned. The new understanding of nature was much more mysterious and almost mystical.

A revolutionary new understanding of nature came to the fore when, in 1905, Albert Einstein pointed out that earlier notions of absolute space and time were metaphysical and were not necessarily rooted in the observations and experiments of science. Time and space are relative to the observer. Light always travels with the same velocity relative to an observer and is the only known constant in the universe. Space is curved and the universe, though vast, is finite. Einstein's conclusions on relativity broke sharply with the old Newtonian, mechanical view of nature where everything, being subject to cause and effect, was predictable and capable of understanding. Einstein compelled men to see the natural universe in a radically new way which often defied the customary canons of reason. The power of science was acknowledged to be limited since only a small portion of nature can be experienced empirically. The rest must be inferred from thought, reflection, and mathematical symbolization. But the conclusions resulting from Einstein's reflections and calculations often seemed absurd, (i.e. time progresses more slowly when one is close to a gravitating body than when there is no gravity or change in speed). Instead of talking about space and time as separate, Einstein talked about events in a complex space-time continuum where space and time must be considered simultaneously. Einstein demonstrated that nature cannot be comprehended fully by man's reason. Man's reason must bow and bend to conform to nature and its incomprehensible, relativistic paradoxes.

Einstein spent a major portion of his later life attempting to reduce all of physics to one basic explanation. He pursued a unified field theory in the endeavor to simplify man's understanding of the physical world. Yet a unification of man's understanding of nature evaded him. In the 20th century, nature is proving to be a mysterious and evasive master which cannot be fully understood by the persons who claim superiority over it.

Early in this century the notion of breaking matter down into energy slowly evolved. Earlier Becquerel had discovered radioactivity. In the first decade of this century radioactivity was traced to the energy contained in atoms. In 1901 Max Planck stated his quantum theory which said radiation is emitted in various sized, indivisible bundles, spurts or quanta. This raised questions for most scientists who had come to believe that light flowed in waves or undulations. Planck was suggesting that light is a stream of particles although there still was a large body of evidence indicating that light travels in waves. Science, henceforth, was forced to live with a paradox which was as perplexing to scientists as the paradox of human free will and divine predestination has been to theologians. The paradox is that light is both corpuscular and undulatory. Nature now has been invested with a certain ambiguity. Natural laws are regarded as mental concepts not concrete realities. In addition, the new quantum mechanics has declared that man may never be able to determine the exact speed, location, and nature of electrons which are basic elements of the physical universe. The nature of energy was beyond man's ability to understand; so Heisenberg declared that the inherent uncertainty concerning the location and velocity of very small objects like electrons is great. Professor Bridgman of Harvard concluded, "the structure of nature may eventually be such that our processes of thought do not correspond to it sufficiently to permit us to think about it all . . . we are now approaching a bound beyond which we are forever stopped from pushing our inquiries, not by the construction of the world, but by the construction of ourselves . . . we are confronted with something truly ineffable."[6] Man is limited in the face of the enormous complexity and mystery of nature.

The ineffable and incredible mystery of nature did not, however, stop scientists. The focus seemed to shift for awhile from seeking to understand nature, which now seemed unknowable, to seeking to release its great power and potential. Scientists by the middle of this century felt their efforts should be directed toward action and technology. Unfortunately, some have failed to recognize that technology without transcendent values can be incredibly destructive. Technological efforts have been buttressed by the thinking of William James, John Dewey and other pragmatists who declared that ideas must result in action, that what works is good.

Consequently, modern science more and more has sought to harness the forces of nature to serve society. Probably 90% of all the scientists who ever have lived are now alive seeking to direct the forces of nature. Vast networks of roads and railroad tracks have made whole continents accessible to man. Jets and space ships have made the skies into part of man's habitat. Nuclear energy has put unlimited power at man's disposal—for good or for ill. Gigantic dams have made water available to vast desert regions. Yet as C.S. Lewis pointed out "every conquest over Nature increases her domain."[7] With each advance that science and technology has made in the 20th century, nature has become more and more important to society. Ironically, technology is being conquered by the nature which it assumes to control. Man, the conqueror of natural forces, has become more and more dependent both upon nature and upon the instruments by which he attempts to subdue and use it. Nature is becoming the conqueror of man.

Nature's greatest victory would be achieved if human beings could be reduced to the level of nature. Nature would be triumphant if, through genetic engineering and operant conditioning, scientists ever should succeed in demonstrating that man is nothing but matter which can be reshaped by scientific processes. Twentieth century science and technology, in their efforts to master all powerful nature, more and more have spread the notion that nature, with man as part of nature, is the source of any values which exist to guide society.

In ages past man saw himself as the center and crown jewel of God's creation. Copernicus demonstrated that he and this spinning planet were not the center of the universe. Darwin showed man he was but a creation of nature. Freud in the 20th century showed man that he was not even rational. Modern technology, computers, automation and robotics are replacing him in the workplace. Sir Francis Crick, B.F. Skinner, and others may deal the coup de grace if they succeed in demonstrating that nature, which man has sought to control, really is his master ready, willing, and able to remake him.

Science in the 20th century unwittingly has made nature all important. Yet it also has demonstrated that nature is not a huge mass of absolutely solid materiality. Matter is a complex combination of electrons, protons, neutrons, positrons and quarks whose substance is unknowable although it is known that they are not solid matter. Terrestrial atoms are open entities containing more empty space than occupied space. Individual atoms are unpredictable. No one knows which radio-active atom will explode next. They cannot be examined because external interference will disturb their structures. Whatever they are, they manifest themselves both as waves and as particles simultaneously. No wonder Einstein said, "In our endeavor to understand reality we are somewhat like a man trying to understand the mechanism of a closed watch . . . He will never be able to compare his picture (his mental construct) with the real mechanism."[8] A mysterious non-solid, non-material universe of nature is the unknowable but very useful master of men in the late 20th century.

As this brief survey suggests, western culture has undergone several major shifts in the values which have undergirded it in the last three millenia. Greek culture evolved from the Creto-Mycanean era, which was predominantly materialistic, to one with predominantly transcendent values (9th–6th c. B.C.). The later Greeks and Romans (3rd c. B.C.–4th c. A.D.) were guided by essentially materialistic values. The Middle Ages (4th through 12th c.) were controlled by transcendent values which eroded with the coming of the Renaissance and the rise of modern thought. The modern era (15th to 20th c.) has been dominated by material, earthbound values although cracks in its materialism may be developing.

Those periods when material values have predominated as well as those periods when transcendent values have held sway have tended to integrate, stabilize, and unify society. People have felt more secure living with values and convictions which are not widely challenged. Transcendent values have tended to lift people toward their higher selves while material values have tended to make people more brutish. In a unified culture, brute force sometimes has been used to maintain the values of the culture. (i.e. The Inquisition and Marxist societies). Nevertheless, cultural unity has prevailed during times when one supersystem of values has dominated society.

Between such periods, there have been transitional periods when earthbound values existed in tension with transcendent values. Old values were fading and new values were emerging. Those have been times when the masses of people were confused and alienated because their minds were battlegrounds for conflicting values. The standards and norms of society were fragmented. Such times have been characterized by outbursts of lawlessness, violence, wars, and revolutions.[9] They have been historical turning points when old values were questioned and when new ones had not yet been accepted as normative. Such eras have been threatening to the masses of people.

Pitrim Sorokin in his monumental study of western culture classified such supersystems of values as sensate (material), ideational (transcendent) and idealistic (a combination of sensate and ideational in the transitional periods). His studies convinced him that during the thirty centuries of Greco-Roman and Western history such major cultural shifts occurred four times. He believed that we in the 20th century are living through one of these revolutionary shifts. He said, "We are seemingly between two epochs: the dying Sensate culture of our magnificent yesterday and the coming Ideational culture of the creative tomorrow."[10] These words were written prior to World War II. Events since that conflagration may indicate that the new Ideational culture of which he spoke has not yet been born, but that a shift within sensate values has occurred. That shift may result from a movement away from man as the pinnacle of nature toward an exaltation of nature as superior to man.

Whether the shift which Sorokin believed was in process is toward a unifying ideational supersystem or whether it is merely a shift within a sensate system remains to be seen. It is possible, however, that if world culture could catch a new vision of transcendence, a new supersystem of values could emerge to usher in an ideational age of unity, harmony and peace. Since we now live in one global community, the new vision of transcendence must be grand enough and universal enough to be meaningful to the peoples of the whole world. To that subject the remainder of this volume will be devoted.

NOTES

[1] Anders Nygren in his motif research pointed out that "a fundamental motif is that which forms the answer given by some particular outlook to a question of such fundamental nature that it can be described in a categorical sense as a fundamental question." Such fundamental questions and answers distinguish one society from another. Cf. *Agape and Eros*, (Philadelphia: Westminster Press, 1953), p. 42.

[2] Eusebius, *Life*, ii, 63, 70.

[3] Randall, John Herman, *The Making of the Modern Mind*, (New York: Columbia University Press, 1976), p. 539.

[4] Rauschenbusch, Walter, *Christianity and the Social Order*, (New York: The MacMillan Co., 1907), p. 565.

[5] Butterfield, Herbert, *The Origins of Modern Science*, (London: G. Bell, 1957), p. vii.

[6] Quoted by James B. Conant, *Modern Science and Modern Man*, (New York: Doubleday Anchor Books, 1953), p.87.

[7] Lewis, C.S., *The Abolition of Man*, (New York: MacMillan, 1975), p.83.

[8] Einstein, Albert and Infeld, Leopold, *The Evolution of Physics*, (New York: Simon and Schuster, 1938), p. 33.

[9] cf. Sorokin, Pitrim, *The Crisis of Our Age*, (New York: E.P. Dutton and Co., 1956), ch. VI. Sorokin, utilizing extensive statistical data, demonstrated that riots, revolutions, and wars have increased dramatically in periods of cultural transition.

[10] Ibid, p. 13.

2

The Church's Struggle to Understand God

Contemporary society is fragmented into many conflicting philosophies and perspectives. In today's world Christian faith is confronted with a hydra-headed naturalism which wears a multitude of faces. Naturalism appears and reappears sometimes as a type of rationalism, sometimes in various forms of romanticism, sometimes as existentialism, and sometimes as scientific materialism. Each expression of naturalism represents an earthbound perspective. Each has its own cultural, social, and political expressions. Each has sufficient truth to make it attractive to its adherents. Yet each also has its limitations and weaknesses. Because most fail to address the whole person (mind, emotions, will), they lack universal appeal to people of varying temperaments and capacities.

In addition, global society is sundered by many different religions. Christianity faces Judaism, Islam, Buddhism, Confucianism, Hinduism, Taoism as well as a multitude of lesser religions and philosophies. Each has something to offer its people. Each is seeking entrance into the souls of humanity. Does anyone of them offer a basis for the unifying of mankind? Except for Christianity, most are so tightly encapsulated by specific cultures that they lack the sense of universality which is necessary to give them worldwide appeal. Most religions of the world lack the capacity to unify a global society.

Christianity itself is fragmented and presently lacks unifying power. There are Roman Catholics, Protestants, Orthodox and a host of lesser denominations. Within Roman Catholicism there are strong divisions. Within Protestantism there is deep alienation. The Orthodox are separated into various national groups.

Is there any Christian truth, common to all, which can bring about a new spiritual unity in Christianity? Is there any vision universal enough and powerful enough to possess and to inspire the hearts and minds of all kinds of Christians everywhere enabling them to become leaven which will leaven the whole global community with values which will unify world culture?

Could it be that a new vision of the God of the Judeo-Christian tradition could have sufficient grandeur, majesty and power to vivify the various forms of the church so that they could lead the way into a new age of spiritual power? At the heart of Christian truth is God Himself. All Christian churches seek to relate themselves to the God who focused Himself in Jesus of Nazareth and who is described in Holy Scripture.

If it is conceivable that a vision of the God of the Judeo-Christian tradition could be the creative dynamic to inspire the churches toward becoming a force moving contemporary society toward a new cultural unity, what form might that vision take? Through the centuries, a common denominator held by most churches is an understanding that the God they worship is Triune. For many living during the Middle Ages, the Trinitarian principle provided inspiration for the unity of society. Could it be that a new understanding and experience of God as Trinity may be able to motivate today's believers to become a spiritual force contributing to a new unity for humankind?

In past ages, what have people in the Biblical tradition understood God to be? Christians have derived their knowledge of God from divine actions in history and primarily from the Christ event of 2000 years ago. Something happened in the hills of Palestine that revolutionized the lives of those involved. One participant in that event stated:

> In the beginning was the Word and the Word was with God and the Word was God . . . And the Word became flesh and dwelt among us, full of grace and truth. (John 1:1,14)

He also wrote:

The Church's Struggle to Understand God

> That which was from the beginning, which we have heard, which we have seen with our eyes, which we have looked upon and touched with our hands, concerning the word of life—the life was made manifest and we saw it, and testify to it, and proclaim to you the eternal life which was with the Father and was made manifest to us. That which we have seen and heard we proclaim also to you, so that you may have fellowship with us; and our fellowship is with the Father and with his Son Jesus Christ. (I John 1:1–3)

This pious, monotheistic Jew, after years of reflecting on the Christ event, was convinced that in Christ someone, who had existed in eternity with God, and who also was God, had come into space/time to live as a human among the Jews in Palestine.

Those early Christians lived and thought in a community that had been shaped largely by Jewish traditions. Many affirmations about the "word" in Hebrew literature suggested that God's Word was hypostasized. (i.e. Gen. 1, Isaiah 55:11, Wisdom 18:15–16) Similarly, Jewish writings implied that Wisdom is personified. (i.e. Proverbs 8:22–31, Wisdom 7:25–26) The conceptual framework of the Jews became the soil in which the New Testament revelation could take root. Jesus was understood to be God's Word and wisdom. The Son of Man expected at the climax of history was understood to be a preexistent heavenly being.[1] The Old Testament also referred to the *Spirit of Yahweh* in personal terms. The Spirit could instruct, guide, refresh, and could be grieved. (Cf. Ps. 143:10, Neh. 9:20, Isa. 63:10,14) Though the Jews did not see a trinity within God, their sacred writings provided the framework, the words, and the intimations which New Testament writers later would use to develop their understanding of a plurality in the Godhead. In this sense, the New Testament revelation was latent in the Old Testament.

Throughout the New Testament, there are recurring references to the Father, Son, and Holy Spirit. For example, Jesus taught His disciples to baptize in the name of the Father, Son, and Holy Spirit. (Matt. 28:19) Paul declared,

> For this reason I bow my knees before the Father . . . that . . . he may grant you to be strengthened with might through His Spirit in the inner man and that Christ may dwell in your hearts through faith. (Eph. 3:14–17)

Peter wrote to those "chosen and destined by God the Father and sanctified by the Spirit for obedience to Jesus Christ and for sprinkling with his blood." (I Peter 1:2) For those monotheistic Jews, who were caught up in an experience of the Spirit of the Risen Christ, to speak and to write of God's divine power in a threefold manner signified that they saw some majestic plurality in the one, great God.

A latecomer to the Christ event, the Apostle Paul, viewed the appearance of the carpenter from Nazareth as God intervening in human affairs to create a new humanity. He spoke of God in Christ adopting humans into the stream of divine life.

> When the time had fully come, God sent forth his Son, born of woman, born under the law, to redeem those who were under the law, so that we might receive adoption as sons, and because you are sons, God has sent the Spirit of his son into our hearts, crying "Abba! Father!" (Gal. 4:4–6)

For Paul heaven had touched earth in Jesus, making possible humanity's adoption into the life of the Father God. He spoke of God's sending His Son to make the new relationship of sonship possible. He also spoke of God's sending His Spirit into human spirits to give a personal knowledge of sonship. According to Paul, the Father, the Son, and the Holy Spirit were involved in humanity's redemption. The redeemed life was life with the Father, made possible by the Son and made effective by the Spirit. It was life "in Christ" and "in the Spirit", and therefore, life with the Father. Though Paul gave no developed doctrine of the Trinity, he provided data for the later statements of the church.

Those believers of New Testament times reveled and rejoiced in their threefold experience of God although they did not endeavor to define specifically and clearly the relationships among Father, Son, and Holy Spirit. Their joyous, doxological experience was so rapturous, exciting, and thrilling that they worshipped and lived in the threeness of God without endeavoring to understand or to define His multiplicity. They exulted in "the grace of the Lord Jesus Christ, the love of God, and the communion of the Holy Spirit" (2 Cor. 13:14) without indulging in abstract, intellectual analysis. Yet their inspired understanding of God was being formed as they pondered the Christ event both against the backdrop of Old Testament revelation and from the perspective of those who had been adopted into the family of God.

Their God was called the "Father in heaven" as taught them by Jesus Christ, the Son of God. Jesus was called the "only begotten" Son as distinct from any other son. Father and Son were present realities in the early church through the presence of the Holy Spirit. The three were presented as mysteriously inter-related, but separated and distinct. The Father was known through the Son. The Son was understood to be the Saviour against the backdrop of the Father's holiness. Both Father and Son were known through the Holy Spirit. The New Testament highlighted these three names as representing three personal identities in the God worshipped by the primitive church.

Descriptions of the three were expressed more by verbs of which God was the Subject than by nouns. The New Testament described their works more than their natures. Their natures later would be inferred from their functions. Jesus sought the lost sheep, proclaimed the Kingdom of God, revealed, reconciled, saved, liberated, healed, mediated, and eventually will judge. The Spirit bore witness, created, filled, taught, prayed, and could be grieved. The Father created, revealed, sent, loved, and promised. God, as the Divine Subject whose actions were described by such verbs had made Himself known in the three who together were the one great God.

As the years passed, the church realized that it was necessary to state its understanding of God more clearly in order to defend itself against teachings which would have destroyed it. The threefold baptismal formula became a kind of creed. The church's devotional experience became transformed into the symbol which was passed down as the Apostles' Creed. It declared belief in "God, the Father Almighty . . . Jesus Christ, his only Son, our Lord . . . the Holy Spirit." The Didache (7:1) called for baptism in the name of the Father, the Son, and the Spirit.

In the first and second centuries, the Apostolic Fathers who echoed the teachings of the Apostles reflected the consciousness of the early church. Among the Apostolic Fathers, there was no developed Trinitarian doctrine. Yet there seemed to be a clear understanding of three divine, pre-existent persons who make salvation possible. With the possible exception of Hermas, all the Fathers acknowledged the divinity of Christ and the Holy Spirit. *The First Letter of Clement* (c. 96,97) spoke of God, the Lord Jesus Christ, and the Holy Spirit: "as God lives, and the Lord Jesus Christ lives, and the Holy Spirit" (58.2) Hermas spoke of the Lord of the farm (Father), the servant (Son), and of human flesh as bearing the Holy Spirit. Though it is unclear whether Hermas was adoptionist or binitarian, he clearly recognized the importance of the Father, Son, and Spirit. Ignatius (c. 110 A.D.) described Christians as stones in the temple of the Father. The stones are carried to the heights by the engine (cross) of Jesus Christ using the rope of the Holy Spirit. (Eph. 9:1) He clearly recognized that Jesus Christ "from eternity was with the Father." (Magn. 6.1) He counseled the Magnesians that "whatever you do may prosper . . . in the Son and Father and Spirit." (*Magn.* 13.2)

Such Trinitarian statements, although not the kerygma, were the result of reflection upon the kerygma. Although the Scriptures did not use the word "Trinity", they described the kerygma in action which gave birth to reflections upon questions raised by the kerygma. Trinitarian statements in the early church were doxologies wrapped in thought.[2] They became necessary as the church, confronted by numerous heresies, began the process of clarifying its beliefs.

The early Apologists of the late 2nd century, in order to defend the church's teaching against Ebionites, Gnostics, and other heretical movements[3] sought to explain the Christian view of God in rational ways. Theophilus of Antioch (c. 180 A.D.) stated "In like manner also the three days, which were before the luminaries, are types of the Triad of God and His Word and His wisdom." (*Ad Autolyeus* 11,15) Athenagoras (c.177), concerned that some apologists seemed to be developing a binary view of God, asked, "What the union and difference of those who are thus united—the Spirit, the Son, and the Father?" He spoke approvingly of "men who speak of God the Father, and of God the Son, and of the Holy spirit and declare both their power in union and their distinction in order." (*Suppl.* 10)

The Apologists often referred to Christ as the Logos of God. This language was familiar to the educated classes who were acquainted with Greek thought in which the Logos occupied a middle position between God and the world. The Stoics thought of the Logos as the divine reason which permeated all of creation. The Apologists gave new meaning to the term following the example of Apostle John. "In the beginning was the Word (Logos) . . ." (John 1:1) John and the Apologists saw the Logos (Word) as begotten of God, as personal and as granted a separate, incarnate mission and existence by the Father. Before His incarnation, He was operative in creation as the Logos who worked in Old Testament prophets and to a lesser degree in all wise, noble persons of the ancient world. This divine reason or Logos, the Apologists saw as revealed perfectly in Christ, the Logos of the Father. The Logos Christology asserted the differentiation of the Father and Son. It was an effort to show how the Son could be different from the Father yet one with Him as God. He was the Word who expressed the Father, who implemented the will of God throughout the universe and who was distinct from the Father although one with Him.

As those Apologists sought to reflect upon the three names, some drifted into a subordinationism which did not recognize adequately a co-equality between the Father and Son. For example, Justin Martyr (c.150) in his *Dialogue* suggested that the Father is God while the Logos is a being of second rank. For him, the Logos became a divine person prior to creation in order to become the Father's instrument of creation. The Son of God as a person is not eternal and infinite. Justin wrote that Christians honor Jesus Christ in the second place after God, and the Spirit in the third place. (1 *Apol.* 13.3) At the same time, he offered worship to all three.

In an effort to preserve monotheism (the unity of God) from

being swallowed up by tritheism, two forms of subordinationism emerged. Each subordinated Jesus Christ to the monarchianism (the sole government) of God. One school (adoptionistic monarchianism) said that Jesus was a man who was adopted by God to become God's son. These held that Jesus was adopted at his baptism when the Holy Spirit fell upon him, that he grew in God and was exalted when God raised him from the dead. A leading adoptionist, Paul of Samosata, described the divine Logos as the influence which equipped the man Jesus to become one with God and which fitted him to become the Redeemer and Son of God. Paul's effort to maintain the unity of God at the expense of Christ's deity was rejected by the church in the third century.

Modalism (modalistic monarchianism) was more widely accepted in the attempt to safeguard monotheism. Although condemned repeatedly by the church, it has persisted to this day. It attempted to maintain the unity of God without sacrificing the deity of Christ. It declared that Christ and the Father were one and that Christ was one of the forms by which the Father revealed himself. Sabellius (c.215) became a leading spokesman for modalism. He believed that Father, Son, and Holy Spirit were three roles played successively by the one divine person. An analogy he used was that a man is body, soul, and spirit, yet he is only one person expressing himself through the three.

Another analogy often employed to illustrate modalism is water. Water is H_2O. Although it may take the form of ice or steam or liquid, it always is H_2O in different modes. Sabellius viewed the one God in three forms, expanding and contracting, as the Father reached out to give the law then fell back into His original form, as the Son reached out in the incarnation then returned at the ascension, as the Holy Spirit expanded into the world then eventually will contract after achieving the perfection of the church. He described Father, Son, and Holy Spirit as one person wearing different masks at different times.

In Alexandria, Clement sought to clarify the Church's understanding of God using categories drawn from Greek philosophy. Clement's notion of God incorporated both Greek and Biblical elements. God was utterly transcendent, incomprehensible and unnameable, but His Logos was His image or mind which was inseparable from Him. The Logos had a personal, pre-existence. He also was identified with the historical Christ. Clement suggested the eternal generation of the Son by the Father and recognized the work of the Holy Spirit. Though Clement's theology did not possess a fully developed understanding of the Triune God, he worshipped the Trinity and declared "One is the Father of all, one also the Logos of all, and the Holy Spirit is one and the same everywhere." (*Paed* 1.6.42.1)

Sharply at odds with Sabellius and other monarchian thinkers, but following after Clement, Origen (d.254) of Alexandria, though neo-Platonic in his conception of God, contributed to the emerging understanding of the Trinity by endorsing an eternal generation of the Son from the Father. The Father always has been begetting the Son. The notion of Christ's pre-existence emphasized His qualitative difference from humanity. From all eternity the Son has been a hypostasis, having a distinct existence. This was an important step toward later statements by the church of the Son's co-eternity and co-equality with the Father. Origen declared that the Holy Spirit also is an eternal hypostasis active in the souls of Christians. Yet Origen retained a hint of subordinationism by calling the Christ a creature, but only in the sense that He is generated by the Father. Origen's struggle to depict the Trinity succeeded in freeing him from the notion of Christ's temporal secondariness, but traces of subordinationism remained because he retained the idea of God as an undifferentiated unity.

Irenaeus, Bishop of Lyon (d.202) opposed the speculations of Gnostics and affirmed forcefully the deity of Jesus Christ. "The Word of God was man from the root of Jesse and . . . He was God" (*Haer* III. 9.3) Irenaeus, in advance of others in the church of the 2nd century, also affirmed the divinity of the Holy Spirit. Though some incorrectly have seen subordinationism and modalism in Irenaeus, he clearly taught that God is eternally Father, Son, and Holy Spirit. He refrained from speculation about the inner life of the Triune God choosing instead to defend the Biblical faith as he understood it.

Tertullian (c.150–225) of North Africa, influenced by Irenaeus' view of Christ as the God-man, pre-existent and co-eternal with the Father, described Father, Son, and Holy Spirit as sharing "one substance, and one essence, and one power" (Adversus *Praxeam*, 2). He spoke of Christ and of the Holy Spirit as God. He declared that the Spirit proceeds from the Father through the Son and is one with them. He coined the word "Trinity" and first used the words "substance" and "person" in describing the relation of Father, Son, and Holy Spirit. He spoke of the one God as a unity which is differentiated. He said the three persons are to each other as a fountain, a stream, and a river. Yet, subordinationism was evident in Tertullian. For him, the Father is the whole divine substance while the Son and Spirit participate in the Father's substance. Along with some Greek Apologists, he held that the hypostasizing of the Son began at the time of creation. (second stage generation) In the recesses of eternity, the Father had existed without the Son. "There was, however, a time when neither sin existed with Him, nor the Son." (*Adv: Hermog.* 3) Though the Logos existed eternally in God, the Logos was not clearly personalized until the time of creation. "Before the establishment of the universe, God was not alone, seeing He continually had in Himself Reason, and in Reason, Word, which He made another beside Himself by activity within Himself." (*Adv. Prax.* 5) The existence of the Son as a distinct person in the Trinity became necessary with the creation of the world. When God's divine plan for the world is fulfilled, the Son and Spirit will return into the oneness of God the Father. For Tertullian, God's oneness overshadows and controls His triunity.

The major problem with which the early church was struggling was how to reconcile the oneness of God with the threeness of God. Biblical revelation had declared clearly that God in Christ was eternal and infinite both before and after His incarnation on earth. Scripture taught that God's Spirit also was eternal and infinite. How could such revelations be reconciled with parallel

Biblical teachings that God was one? Throughout the church there was widespread adoration of Christ as divine. But what did that mean in the face of Biblical teaching that God is one?

The confusion arose largely because of the church's conception of the oneness of God. The ancients, like many moderns, conceived the unity of God as mathematical. They thought of unity as simple, undifferentiated and without internal complexity or multiplicity. One plus one always equals two. What is one never can be two, nor can that which is two ever be one. It implied a fixity and rigidity of oneness which ignored the possibility of either an aesthetic or an organic unity beyond mere numerical unity.

For example, the aesthetic unity of Michelangelo's *Pieta* is composed of many parts. The unity of the human self or of the human body also is composed of many interacting parts. Numerical unity is only one type of unity. Each unity is capable of division into smaller parts. A stone can be broken down into its chemical constituents. Those chemical components in turn can be broken down into atoms containing electrons, protons, and neutrons. Each unity contains its parts. As the ancient debates over the one and the many made clear, the One contains the many even as the many make possible the One. Therefore, those who viewed God as one in a strictly numerical sense were ignoring the possibility that God's eternal oneness might contain an eternal diversity and multiplicity.

The Apologists struggled with God's threeness in oneness. Some resorted to various forms of subordinationism in an effort to maintain the notion of a mathematical oneness in God. It was not until later that Christian thinkers came to consider that unity in God may be the result of an intense, eternally binding relationship of self-giving love among three divine personalities. Later it would become apparent that the only perfect unity is in God and that God's oneness is infinitely complex, infinitely beyond the simple arithmetical unity assumed by many in the early church.

Yet the church struggled on to fathom the God revealed in Christ. Clarification resulted from the fierce debate which erupted between two young priests in Alexandria, Egypt. Arius, through his teacher Lucian of Antioch, had been influenced by Paul of Samosata. Like Paul, Arius rejected modalism in favor of another subordinationist view which saw the Logos-Christ as an independent being who was more than man but less than God. Arius taught a real, essential difference between the Father and the Son. He said, "The Unbegun made the Son a beginning of things originated; and advanced Him as a Son to Himself by adoption. He has nothing proper to God in proper subsistence. For He is not equal, nor one in essence with Him." (*Thalia* cited by Athanasius) The Father is God while the Son is a creature who, though pre-existent before time and space, once did not exist. God created the Son and destined Him to be the instrument of cosmic creation. The Son or Logos was a finite creature who nevertheless was perfect. The Father was an undifferentiated unity who was unable to create the cosmos without the mediation of a created being who was above and beyond the universe. The Father created the Son to mediate in the creation of the world. Arius' admission that the Father needed a mediator to effect creation underscored the fact that a solitary, undifferentiated deity was an absolute who not only could not create by Himself, but also could not love because He was a totally self-contained and self-sufficient monad.[4] Arianism, consequently, was a strange mixture of adoptionism with an Origenistic doctrine of a subordinate Logos.

Alexander, the bishop of Alexandria, at a synod held at Alexandria in 321 A.D. excommunicated Arius for his views. Eusebius of Nicomedia supported Arius. Eusebius of Caesarea, while not agreeing with Arius, wanted to tolerate him. Division spread through the church. To resolve the strife, Emperor Constantine convened the church's first General Council in 325 A.D. at Nicea. About 318 bishops attended, among them Alexander and his archdeacon Athanasius.

Eusebius of Nicomedia proposed a creed which was thoroughly Arian, but it was firmly voted down. Eusebius of Caesarea then proposed a compromise creed calling Christ the "created image", but Alexander and Athanasius opposed it.

Then Emperor Constantine's trusted advisor, Hosius of Cordova, recommended that the word homoousios (the same nature or substance) be applied to Christ. So the creed of Eusebius of Caesarea was modified to read: "We believe in one God, the Father Almighty, maker of all things visible and invisible. And in one Lord Jesus Christ, the Son of God, begotten of the Father, only begotten, i.e., *of the same nature/substance (homoousios) of the Father*. God of God, Light of Light, very God of very God, begotten not created, of one substance with the Father . . ." The Council of Nicea often has been criticized because it used a Greek notion (i.e. substance) to describe the God of the Bible. Yet, Arius had raised an ontological question. Therefore, the Council felt obliged to transpose Biblical teachings into ontological terminology. This it endeavored to do by responding to Arius' ontological question with an ontological answer. The Son is consubstantial with the Father. In addition, an anathema was added: "But the holy and apostolic church anathematizes those who say that there was (a time) when he was not, and that he was made from things not existing, or from another person or being, saying that the Son of God is mutable or changeable." So the Nicean creed was drafted. It was signed by all except Arius and a few others.

The debate made it clear that Arianism tended toward polytheism. Its view of Christ made him a demigod who is to be adored, along with the Father, while he does not essentially differ from other creatures.

On the other hand, Athanasius' belief in the co-eternity and co-equality of the Son and the Father was affirmed. Nicea stressed the Son's relation to the Father. The Holy Spirit was merely mentioned. Yet, Athanasius in his *Letters to Serapion* insisted that the Holy Spirit belongs to the "holy Triad" and "is not a creature." The relative silence of Nicea on the Holy Spirit should not be interpreted as an affirmation of His being less than God. The question at Nicea was "Who is Christ?" The basis for man's redemption was being debated. Nicea affirmed that in Christ, God Himself has redeemed mankind. To accomplish this, God in Jesus Christ entered the stream of humanity. The

Logos, viewed as the rational principle of creation, had been rejected in favor of God the Son, the Redeemer.

But the victory of Nicea was short-lived. The Arians and neo-Origenists (Eusebius of Caesarea) continued to challenge the Athanasian view. Athanasius was exiled five times, persecuted and oppressed. Councils were called (Sardica—343; Antioch—344; Milan—345–347) which reiterated the orthodox views, but which demanded the deposition of Athanasius and Marcellus of Ancyra. Although Arians and semi-Arians continued to be vocal, the final triumph of Athanasius took place at the Council of Constantinople (381)[5] which affirmed the homoousios of the three Persons.

Contributing significantly to the victory of Nicene theology in the church were the three great Cappadocians, Basil of Caesarea, his brother Gregory of Nyssa, and Gregory of Nazianzus. Unlike Athanasius, who stressed one God with a threefold personal life, they emphasized three divine hypostases possessing one nature. Athanasius began with the one divine nature encompassing three eternal persons. The Cappadocians, along with later Greek theologians began with three divine persons in one divine substance. They interpreted Athanasius in the light of the Logos Christology of Origen. They retained the notion of an impersonal substance which always has threatened the full personality of God, and which for some has suggested a fourth mode of divine existence. They also spoke of the generation of the Word as having some relation to the Father's mind though they did not suggest that the generation of the Son was by way of the intellect. Later Western theologians would use the intellectual relation of the Word to the Father's mind to explain why the Son is generated by the Father and the Holy Spirit is not.

The Athanasian view of the Holy Spirit as homoousious (co-essential, same-natured) with the Father and the Son was affirmed at a synod at Alexandria (362), later by the Cappadocians and then by the Council of Constantinople (381). The difference between the Son and the Spirit was declared to be that the Son is generated and sent forth while the Spirit proceeds.

The victory of Athanasius' views in the West was established by the impressive work of Augustine. Like Athanasius, his starting point was the unity of God who possesses one substance, one nature, one energy and one will. Each person of the Trinity, in respect to the divine substance, is equal to the others and to the whole divine substance. Augustine said of the God who eternally unfolds Himself in three persons, "they are infinite in themselves. And so each is in each, all are in each, each is in all, all are in all and all are one." (*De Trin.* VI, 10.12) He wrote, "For Father and Son and Holy Spirit together are not a greater essence than the Father alone or the Son alone, but these three substances or persons, if they be so called, are together equal to each one alone." (*De Trin.* VII, 6.11) The divine unity and personhood are inseparably linked in Augustine's thought. God's unity is a *personal* unity. There is a mutual inner relationship among Father, Son, and Spirit. They have one will. "The will of the Father and the Son is one and their operation inseparable." (*De Trin.* II,9)

A key concept which Augustine contributed to theological thought about the Trinity was relationship. "The names, Father and Son, do not refer to the substance, but to the relation." (*De Trin* V,6) The relationships which distinguish one person from another are unchangeable and eternal. The Father is always begetting. The Son is always being born. The Spirit is always being given or proceeding from the Father and Son. There is no more ultimate reality than the God of personal relationships. God *is* His attributes and relations. Father, Son, and Spirit each require the others. Each is dependent upon the others. Each contains the entire deity, but each is deity from a different point of view. (generating, generated, spirated) Each interpenetrates and indwells the others. Each *is* His attributes.

Misunderstanding has arisen from Augustine's using the analogy of lover, beloved, love to describe the Trinity. If the Holy Spirit is the love which unites the Father and the Son, is the Holy Spirit an influence, energy, something less than personal? Augustine makes it eminently clear that the Spirit is personal in the same sense that Father and Son are personal. Speaking of the Spirit, Augustine said, "He is God in Himself . . . for before He was given to anyone He was God coeternal with the Father and the Son. Nor because They give and He is given is He less than They. For as God's Gift, He is given in such a way that He Himself is God the Giver" (*De Trin.* XV, 36) It seems unreasonable to infer from a passing reference to lover, beloved, love (*De Trin.* VI, 7) that Augustine viewed the Spirit as less than personal since His whole argument is that Father, Son, and Holy Spirit are three persons, co-equal and co-eternal.

Augustine, however, was not content with describing Father, Son, and Spirit as "persons." "Person" is a word which we use to describe humans. It is inadequate to depict the Infinite who cannot adequately be described either by words or by comparisons to that which is finite. He explained, "Yet we say three persons, not in order to express it, but in order not to be silent." (*De Trin.* V,9,10)

Realizing the inadequacies of human thought to comprehend the Infinite God, Augustine nevertheless sought to illustrate the Trinity by analogies drawn from the human soul. He spoke of a trinity in sight (the seen, vision itself, and the will uniting them), a trinity in the human spirit (mind or self-knowledge, self-love or self-esteem, and will), and a trinity in love (the lover, the loved, love itself). Such analogies illustrate that three can be one. Yet Augustine was acutely aware of the limitations and insufficiency of his analogies.

Augustine's vision of the Trinity deeply affected both church and society in the years that followed. Augustine's vision of the society that was to be was profoundly affected by his theological presuppositions. Graeco-Roman society had been based upon the notions of the ultimacy of impersonal being or of anthropomorphic deities or of nature. The self-perfectibility of man and of society was to be accomplished largely through rational and political means. Augustine dramatically called for a new society based upon a personal God who is Trinity. Corresponding to the redemptive "Trinitarian principle" which would be the source, inspiration and basis of his new society, Augustine forcefully reaffirmed the Biblical teaching of man's finiteness, sinfulness and inability to perfect himself apart from the grace of the Triune

God. Augustine denied the perfectibility of man or of society apart from God's grace.

The Trinitarian principle, however, offered hope to a society of despairing people. It offered unity to a divided society. It offered creativity to a society drugged by its own selfishness. It offered cosmic personhood to counter the depersonalization of humanity. So, Augustine called for a radical revision of the first principles and presuppositions of society. He called for a change from classical, naturalistic, autonomous principles to Trinitarian principles.

In both *De Trinitate* and the *Civitas Dei,* Augustine strongly and clearly had identified himself with Nicean (Athanasian) Christianity. In *De Trinitate*, Augustine declared:

> "We have alrcady observed that the only terms which can strictly be applied to distinguish the several persons of the Trinity are those which denote their mutual relations: Father, Son, and Holy Spirit, Gift of both."

Note Augustine's emphasis on the Trinity of relationships in God. Augustine pointed out that the relations of the three persons in God differentiates them without affecting the "substantial" unity, existence and equality of the three eternal persons. . .

> "Thus the Father is God, the Son God, the Holy Spirit God; the Father is good, the Son good, the Holy Spirit good; the Father almighty, the Son almighty, the Holy Spirit almighty; yet there are not three Gods or three good or three almighty; but one God, good, almighty—the Trinity itself . . ."

Each person possesses the whole substance of the Godhead.

> "In this Trinity there is an absolute equality. In divinity the Father is not greater than the Son; nor are the Father and the Son greater than the Holy Spirit; nor is any single person of the three anything less than the Trinity itself." (Book VIII,l)

> "Let us believe that Father, Son and Holy Spirit are one God, maker and ruler of the whole creation: that Father is not Son, nor Holy Spirit Father or Son; but a Trinity of mutually related persons, and a unity of equal essence." (Book IX,l,i)

In *Civitas Dei,* Augustine continued his Trinitarian emphasis:

> We believe, maintain and faithfully teach that the Father begot the Word, that is, the only begotten Son who is the Wisdom by which all things were created. He is one as the Father is one, eternal as the Father is eternal, and equally with the Father, is supremely good. The Holy Spirit is, likewise, the Spirit of the Father and of the Son, consubstantial and co-eternal with both . . . yet, when we ask concerning each person individually, the answer must be that each one is God and each is Almighty; and when we inquire concerning the three together, the reply must be that there are not three Gods or three Almighties, but a single God Almighty. (Book XI, ch. 24)

Augustine, in such statements, clearly repudiated Arianism (which said the Son was subordinate to and created by the Father) and Sabellianism (which declared that Father, Son, and Holy Spirit were each transitory, temporary manifestations or masks worn by the one great God). He identified himself with Nicean Christianity.

Having delineated his overarching, theological first principle, Augustine showed the benefits which the Trinitarian principle offered mankind. He contrasted these benefits to the failure and impotence of classic, Graeco-Roman first principles centering either in impersonal being or in anthropomorphic gods or in nature.

The Trinitarian principle accomplished what Plato could not do. Plato had attempted to reconcile the Parmenidean concept of unchanging being with the Heracleitean notion of constantly changing becoming. Material things in the realm of becoming "participated" in ideas which belonged to the transcendent realm of being. Yet, Plato never really succeeded in relating or unifying being and becoming.

For Augustine, the Trinity unified all reality in a way that Greek and Roman philosophy had not. For example, Plato talked of being. Augustine talked of God the Father as the source of all being. Plato talked of becoming and the world of matter. Augustine spoke of God the Holy Spirit who undergirds, supports, and gives continuous existence to all creation. Plato spoke of "participation." Augustine spoke of God the Son who in the unity of the Trinity linked together invisible and visible reality. The three in one God encompassed, undergirded and unified all of reality. Essence and existence united in the Triune God.

Charles N. Cochrane in his monumental *Christianity and Classical Culture*, speaking of Augustine's view of one God in three persons said, "In this formula the first hypostasis, Being, the creative principle properly so called is, strictly speaking, unknown and unknowable, except insofar as it manifests itself in the second and third; the second hypostasis, the principle of intelligence, reveals itself as the logos, ratio, or order of the universe; while the third, the hypostasis of spirit, is the principle of motion therein." (p. 410) Cochrane in striking fashion shows how Augustine's Trinity unifies all reality in a way that Plato's concepts of being, participation and becoming could not. Augustine saw the Trinity unifying all reality while preserving a dynamic, creative sense of order in the universe. Plato failed because his ultimate (being) was transcendent but lacked immanence. Consequently it failed to unify the invisible and visible realms. The Trinity was both transcendent and immanent, unifying and ordering all reality by the dynamic threeness-in-oneness which undergirded the manyness and oneness of the universe.

Cochrane also pointed out that "Augustine thus discovers in the Trinity a fresh foundation for what we have called the values of personality. And here the breach with Classicism was radical . . ."(p. 410) Plato saw reality in terms of impersonal form (being) and matter (becoming). Augustine saw divine personality overarching, undergirding and permeating all reality. Ultimate reality was personal, therefore, personal values were exalted and made determinative for society. That which dehumanizes and violates the sacredness of personality is evil. Man now could be delivered from the tyranny of nature. Man was not just an extension of nature. He was a person created in the image of God. The Trinity who ruled over nature could exalt man above nature. Belief in the Trinitarian God dethroned the classical, impersonal concepts of fortune and fate which had led to the notion that the state was predestined to control man and to monopolize physical and economic power. The personal God exalted man who was made in his image. The Trinitarian perspective undercut impersonal, classical ideas and offered man both an open universe ruled by personality and a society in which free men could live out a new humanity as persons made in the image of the divine Persons. Augustine saw the divine personality providing fulfillment of the classical dream by its exaltation of human personality. Thus, it provided a dynamic, philosophic basis for a new humanism.

The Trinitarian principle also was seen as creative and comprehensive. It is the dynamic and creative power which recreates and redeems fallen humanity by grace. It recreates the human personality by meeting the needs of the whole person. Head and heart are satisfied by reason and faith, which become instruments of God's revelation. Thus they work in magnificent harmony with each other. The whole person; body, mind, and spirit, are recreated and unified by the recreating power of the Triune God. In turn, whole, recreated people become the building blocks of a whole, recreated society.

The new humanity made possible by God's grace is capable of knowing and practicing love and justice in society. Apart from God's revealed justice and love, human justice and love have no content and drift on the sea of life lacking absolute and unchanging authority. Absolutes are known only as the Triune God reveals what absolute justice and love are. "True justice is not to be found save in that commonwealth . . . whose Founder and Ruler is Jesus Christ." (*C.D.*II,21) The revelation of the Triune God in Scripture, received by faith seeking understanding, makes possible reliable and unchanging standards by which society can and must live. Christ, the Incarnate God, revealed the way society can be liberated from cyclically repeating the defeats and failures of the past. Christ, the second person of the Trinity, is both the revelation of how mankind is to live and the goal toward which linear history is to move. He is the Incarnation of love and justice.

Augustine also saw in the Trinity the power whereby society can accomplish some measure of the good life (i.e. God's will) on earth. Cochrane declared "The doctrine of sin and grace marks, in its most acute form, the breach between Classicism and Christianity." (p.451) The Greeks believed in man's self-perfectibility which, because society is "man writ large," means the self-perfectibility of society. For the Greeks autonomous man, through his own reason and intelligence, was clever enough to save and to perfect society. Yet the facts belied the theory. Society in Augustine's day was foundering. Man had proved himself incapable either of creating or of sustaining a perfect society. Man's selfishness and sin have caused every society eventually to run aground and to destroy itself. The grace of the Triune God, Augustine said, was needed both to motivate and to guide society. So Augustine took sharp issue with Pelagius and the Greek tradition of self-perfectibility. (cf. *C.D.* XIX,25) Only the grace of Christ can redeem people so that they can form a Christian society. Only through grace can the classical yearnings and ideals be realized. Without the grace of the Triune God, society fails to fulfill its dreams. Thus Augustine answered those who were asking "why" the Roman Empire fell. Without the cleansing, regenerating power of Christ, decay and corruption had overwhelmed and destroyed Rome.

By his Trinitarian understanding, Augustine also highlighted the two-edged principle of unity and division which always has existed in human history. Christ's truth and values are not just for Jew or Roman or Scythian but are for all men since they arise from the will of the one, universal God. They unite men in God. At the same time, Christ's truth and values divide men, the righteous from the unrighteous. (*C.D.* XIX,17)

The twin principles of unity and division were described by Augustine in the two societies or cities described in *Civitas Dei*. The City of God is peopled by those who love the Triune God while the city of the world is peopled with those who love self, the world, and the devil. These two cities check and balance each other in society. The City of God keeps the city of the world from destroying the earth by its fleshly desires and appetites. The City of God is the "salt of the earth" preserving society even in the midst of corruption and evil desire. The whole human race from the beginning to the end of time is divided either into those who are citizens of God's Kingdom or those who are citizens of the Devil's Kingdom.

> "That which animates secular society is the love of self to the point of contempt for God; that which animates divine society is the love of God to the point of contempt for self." (*C.D.*XIV,28)

What was important to Augustine were the attitudes and loves of the people of the two cities. Augustine defined the state as a "group of rational beings, associated on the basis of a common tie in respect of those things which they love." (*C.D.* XIX,24)

The attitude of the secular city was possessive and greedy. Its citizens' desire to possess arose from a love of material things which serve the love of self. The city of the world is characterized by a struggle for survival. "This world is a sea wherein men devour one another in turn like fish." Thus, the city of the world is full of fear mingled with a longing for security. Fear of enemies outside induces a certain cohesion within the state. Yet, Augustine pointed out that fear is a negative and inadequate basis for social peace and order. But conflict is an inevitable element of life in the city of the world.

Belief in the existence of the pagan gods was attributed to society's desires both to justify its own self-love *and* to preserve itself in the midst of a danger filled world.

> "It is the peculiarity of secularism that it worships a god or gods, by whose aid it may reign victorious in temporal peace, animated not with the love of wise counsel but with the lust for possession. For the good use this world in order that they may enjoy God; but the evil use God in order that they may enjoy this world." (*C.D.* XV,7)

The basic weakness of the Greeks and Romans was, then, their failure to identify the true source of power and to perceive its nature. The pagan gods had no power to save society. The fall of Rome occurred because its gods were powerless to save society from the greed and selfishness which had saturated every aspect of its life.

The Christian, however, as a citizen of the City of God

recognizes the source of power as the Trinity, revealing love and justice to the world. The city of the world exalts the love of power. The City of God exalts the power of love. Grace and love set men free. Thus, God-revealed truth and values are exalted in the City of God whereas man-made truth and values are exalted in the city of the world. The city of the world creates a naturalistic world view which sees things as either one, big, autonomous machine (materialism) or as one, big, autonomous soul (idealism). The City of God, in response to the revealing of the Triune God, sees the world as unified, as finite, as created, as sustained by the living and true God upon whom it is wholly dependent.

The sinfulness and selfishness of mankind is restrained in the City of God by man's conversion, regeneration and obedience to the Triune God. The state is seen not as the ultimate form of community described by Greeks and Romans but as an instrument of regulating the external relations of humanity. The state exists to restrain evil and to encourage goodness. The state, however, is unable to eliminate evil. Only God can do that. Augustine thus rejected the pretensions of the state to become God. It exists to check the power of human sin.

Augustine offered the world a fresh vision of society. He offered a vision of society which called men to work, to pray, to fight for the actualization of God's will upon earth. The vision of the City of God is a prospect which can fulfill humanity. Society in the City of God was to be based on faith in the supernatural, Triune God. The society so constituted would be one body in Christ. It would be as inclusive as the human race. It would not be totalitarian. It would be a free community whose members are set free from sin by grace and wherein all freely love and serve God. Thus Augustine deprived the state of its supremacy and pointed to the human will, adopted, redeemed, and sanctified by the Triune God, as the foundation of society. His social order was derived from the human personality which was set free by the Triune God. His vision of the City of God was distinct from the visible church. The visible church includes lovers of God as well as lovers of the world. The City of God includes only those who love God. It encompasses many in the visible church and many more. The City of God includes all who are the invisible church, all who truly love and serve God whether or not they be in the visible church. The City of God is a present supernatural reality in the midst of humanity. It coexists in time with the naturalistic, autonomous city of the world. The present society is made up of an intermingling of citizens of the two cities. The final separation will come in eternity. Then and only then the City of God will be perfected. But the city of the world will never be perfected. Human sin precludes that possibility. Until the perfection of the City of God in eternity, the City of God and the city of the world will coexist and interpenetrate each other, "both alike enjoying temporal goods and suffering temporal evils, but with a faith that is different, a hope that is different, a love that is different." (*C.D.* XVIII,54) Until the final fulfillment in eternity, the City of God will seek lovingly and justly the ascendancy of the good over the evil in society.

So, from his Trinitarian theological presupposition Augustine derived a vision of the society that was to come, the City of God. It was a creation of the Triune God. From his epistemological presupposition, which exalted God's revelation both through Scripture and through God's illuminating Spirit, Augustine was given a vision of God's love and justice. God was to be the Teacher of individuals and of society. From his anthropology which saw man as corrupt, selfish, greedy, and sinful, he derived an explanation for the fall of the city of the world, of empires like Babylon and Rome. Yet his anthropology also included a vision of the converted, redeemed humanity which was possible through the grace of the Triune God. That new humanity makes up the City of God where justice and love reign. The traits of the City of God will be humility, unity, peace, and the life of the spirit. In time and space, the City of God helps to check the sin of the city of the world. It is the stabilizing force keeping society from committing mass suicide. The City of God also provides humanity with a vision of the future. It provides hope. It offers an alternative to the selfish, destructive, fear-filled city of the world. It was and is the hope and the vision of a society which can fulfill humanity's yearnings and dreams in time as well as in eternity. But it is a supernatural city, whose source is the Triune God and whose perfection will be *fully* realized only in eternity.

Augustine's Trinitarian views later were reflected and incorporated in the Athanasian creed or Quicunque Vult (named for its opening words). Although Athanasius had no connection with the creed which bears his name, by about 500 A.D. that creed was widely known. While the Nicene creed (325 A.D.) contained a trace of subordinationism in that it could be interpreted that the Son and Spirit only participate in the divine substance by virtue of their derivation from the Father, the Quicunque Vult expressly declared that "the whole three persons are co-eternal together; and co-equal." It clearly rejected subordinationism once and for all. It came to control the interpretation of the creeds of Nicea and Constantinople for the Western church, particularly after the powerful Franks converted (c.496) to its understanding of Christianity.

Another facet of the development of Trinitarian doctrine dealt with the Holy Spirit. The western church, influenced by Augustine, understood the Holy Spirit to proceed not only from the Father, but also from the Son. (filioque) At some point, "filioque" unofficially had been inserted into the Nicene creed. The Synod of Aachen (809) accepted this addition. It became the official version of the Nicene creed in the West though never in the East. This sharp difference later led to separation of the Eastern and Western churches in 1054—a separation which continues to this day.

The Niceno-Constantinopolitan creed[6] avoided any statement about either the Son's involvement with the procession of the Spirit from the Father or the relationship of the Son and Spirit. It spoke of the procession of the Spirit from the Father apparently in order to assert the full deity of the Spirit just as it had spoken of the full deity of the Son. Yet it should not be assumed that the church, by its silence in the earlier creeds rejected the Son's participation in the Spirit's procession. Earlier statements by the Cappadocians, for example, interpreted the Spirit as "the Spirit of the Son" and "the Spirit of Christ."

Certainly the Western church both before and after the insertion of the "filioque" did not view the Son and Father as competing in the procession of the Spirit. The Western and Eastern churches agreed that the Holy spirit proceeds from the Father (cf. John 15:26). Only the Western church, however, added "filioque" to underscore the full deity both of the Son who participates in the Spirit's procession and of the Spirit who receives of the fullness of the Father and Son.

Through the centuries, Christian thinkers continued to elaborate and develop the doctrine of the Trinity. Boethius (d.c.525) applied Aristotelian categories to the doctrine and so laid a foundation on which Scholastics would build later. The Council of Toledo (675 A.D.) stressed the distinctions and the inseparability of the divine persons. Anselm of Canterbury (d.1109), using Scripture and reason, defended the "filioque." In analyzing the plurality in God, he found "insociable relations" among Father, Son, and Holy Spirit. Father, Son, and Holy Spirit are one except where some opposition or tension in their relations creates a distinction. The relation of Father and Son are relations which are in opposition since the Father cannot be Son nor Son the Father. Later, Joachim of Flora (d. 1202) divided world history into three epochs. The era under the law was the age of the Father. The era following the Gospel was the age of the Son. The era under the growth of spiritual knowledge and the divinization of humanity was the age of the Holy Spirit. Joachim's tendency toward Tritheism, suggested by the sharp distinctions he made among the three persons, was denounced by the Fourth Lateran Council (1215).

Thomas Aquinas (d.1274) sought to probe the relations in God. He saw the divine nature as intellectual. In spite of Athanasius' warning against rational probing into the nature of the generation of the Son and the procession of the Holy Spirit and in spite of Augustine's saying they were insoluble mysteries, Thomas sought to analyze generation and procession. He saw generation as an act which produces one's likeness. It is, according to Thomas, an intellectual act which brings forth the Father's Word. On the other hand, the procession of the Holy Spirit is an operation of the divine will which issues in love. Thus, Thomas clearly differentiated between generation and procession in God. (*Summa Theologica* Ia,27) He also pointed out that the divine names derive from relations in the Godhead. Paternity, filiation, spiration, procession represent relations between the Father and Son, the Father and the Spirit. The persons are distinct from one another because of their mutual "opposition." (*ST* Ia, 28) So, following Boethius, he wrote that a divine person is "a relationally distinct subsistent in the divine essence." (*ST* Ia, 29.1) Thomas' metaphysical exploration of the Trinity for a long while held sway in the Dominican order. He represents the peak of speculation about the Trinity.

The medieval church's formulation of its trinitarian faith reached a high water mark at the Council of Florence (1438–1445) which was convened to restore the unity of Eastern and Western churches. East and West were sharply divided over the filioque. The lengthy debate brought the participants to see that saying the Holy Spirit proceeds *from* the Son (Western Church) is tantamount to saying He proceeds *through* the Son (Eastern Church). So they agreed that "the Holy Spirit proceeds from the Father through the Son" and agreed on the inclusion of filioque in the creed. The understandings begun at Nicea now were extended and established throughout the whole church by the last General Council to deal with Trinitarian dogma. Unfortunately, when the Greeks returned home, they quickly rejected their agreement, an action which has been ascribed to pressure from the Emperor.

As the Protestant Reformation erupted into European life, Luther, Calvin, and their followers affirmed traditional Trinitarian doctrines. They particularly appreciated Augustine's explication of Trinity though they emphasized the Biblical views of the three persons in God.

So the church's understanding of the Triune God had developed across the centuries. It had pointed medieval society toward the transcendent, personal God who humanized and personalized reality. It had inspired and comforted the masses. But then the reality of the Trinitarian vision slowly began to fade as economic interests replaced religious interests with the rise of trade and exploration as well as with the emergence of large, busy urban areas. The Triune vision began to fade as the Renaissance shifted society's focus toward man. Men began to search for answers to their ultimate questions in the empirical sciences and humanistic philosophies. The coup de grace to Trinitarianism came when many churches in the West, under the influence of Kant, Schleiermacher, Hegel, and others, sought to reinterpret the notion of the Trinity according to secular notions and categories.

Like the Gnostics of old, many theologians of the 18th, 19th and 20th centuries allowed philosophy to absorb and to distort historic Christian doctrines including the Trinity. In the 18th century subjectivism let loose by Kant and Schleiermacher allowed the autonomous human mind and feelings to distort the church's understanding of the Trinity. Immanuel Kant (1724–1804) spurned divine revelation making knowledge of the Trinity impossible. Since God could not be empirically experienced, and since the infinite could not be sifted through the rational structures of the human mind, the best Kant could offer was a postulate about God. The postulate was based upon man's subjective experience of the categorical imperative. The postulate of God emerged from human subjectivity.

For Schleiermacher, God was the reality which corresponded to man's feeling of complete dependence. He was not clear on whether or not the divine reality was personal. His Trinitarianism was based on religious feeling and nothing else. It had a very tenuous relation to historical events such as the Resurrection. It tended toward a modalism of the divine being which manifests itself in Christ and in the church. Traditional Trinitarianism to him seemed to border on tritheism. He abandoned the preexistence of Jesus and saw Christ as an archetype or pattern for humanity instead of as incarnate deity. Jesus' God consciousness inspires humanity to share in God consciousness, but He Himself is not God.

In the 19th century idealist thinkers, although exalting personality, reverted to a type of Greek Logos doctrine when they taught that the self-expression of the Absolute is tantamount to the Father's expressing Himself through the Logos principle of creation. For Fichte and Hegel, God as absolute was not viewed as substance, but as the perfect subject who is known only in man's own self-knowledge. "God", Hegel wrote, "is God only insofar as He knows Himself."[7] His self knowledge is His self consciousness in man. God only has reality in the minds of those who believe. Only the rational is real. God the Father is pure abstract idea. God the Son is its going over into finite being. For Hegel, the second person of the Trinity is finite being. God the Spirit is its returning back to its source. Hegel's Trinity had no reality apart from the finite creation. It was vastly different from the church's historic understanding of God. History was the story of God's becoming and evolving. God was abstract idea in motion. Later, Adolf von Harnack (1851–1930) saw in the church's description of the Trinity an unacceptable hellenization and distortion of the original Christian teaching. So the stage was set for a 20th century revival of modalism which proclaimed one divine subject in different modes of being.

Karl Barth, starting from the sovereignty and unity of the one divine Subject, equated God's sovereignty with God's essence or nature. The Trinity was a means of establishing and expressing that sovereignty. The Trinity emphasized the strict unity and single essence of God. The one divine subject reveals His rule through His Triuneness and His subjectivity. Barth perceived God as one personal God in the mode of the Father, in the mode of the Son, in the mode of the Spirit (veiling, unveiling and impartation). God is the eternal, threefold repetition of one and the same personal God. If, above all else, God is Lord (sovereign), all His activity proceeds from the Father who is the one divine personality. The Son becomes God's otherness in which God contemplates Himself, becomes conscious of Himself, and reveals Himself. The Son really has no independent self-consciousness. Barth called the Trinity "Christian monotheism." Influenced by Idealist philosophy, Barth developed a concept of the unity and sovereignty of God which was based on his analysis of revelation. It brought him close to historic Trinitarian doctrine.

Barth profoundly influenced 20th century Christianity. Many Protestant and Roman Catholic theologians (i.e. Karl Rahner) adopted his views. Many in the churches of the 20th century, under the influence of Schleiermacher, Hegel, Barth, process theologians who went beyond Hegel, Rudolph Bultmann who viewed traditional views of the Word and Spirit as mystical, and Paul Tillich who declared that Jesus Christ "is certainly not God Himself."[8] began to lose the vision of the Trinity which could bring new life to the churches and unity to the culture in which they ministered. For many centuries, Christians had an awareness of three divine persons who overshadowed and undergirded their lives. The ultimacy of persons who gave meaning to society had a humanizing, unifying effect on the social order. Now that awareness has faded. The time is ripe for the church to recapture a renewed vision of the Triune God who can save a fragmented humanity and a foundering civilization.

NOTES

[1] Cf. Daniel 7:13–14; Proverbs 8:22ff.; Enoch 39:6, 40:5, 42:1–3; Syr. Baruch, ch. 29.

[2] Cf. Helmut Thielecke, *The Evangelical Faith* v.2, (Grand Rapids: William B. Eerdmans, 1977), p. 174.

[3] Ebionites denied the virgin birth and believed that Jesus was only a man who received the Holy Spirit (a female spirit) for the first time at his baptism. Gnosticism distinguished Christ (a spiritual emanation) from the man Jesus. The Christ had joined himself temporarily to the man Jesus and left him before the crucifixion. The Christ had no body. (Docetism)

[4] Cf. Migliore, Daniel L. *Called To Freedom,* Westminster Press, Philadelphia, 1980, p. 70. Dr. Migliore points out that "For Arius, God is absolute, utterly transcendent, totally free, completely unconditioned power . . . In short, Arius upheld the 'infinite qualitative difference' between God and humanity . . . But the God of Arius cannot love."

[5] The present form of the Nicene Creed, called the Niceno-Constantinopolitan creed, is not identical either with the Nicene creed of 325 or with the creed delivered by the Council of Constantinople (381). Rather, it probably is a modification of the Baptismal Formula used at Jerusalem into which were

woven phrases from Nicea along with statements about the Holy Spirit. Cf. footnote 6.

⁶ This creed was read and received at the Council of Chalcedon (451) as representing the thought of the 318 fathers who met at Nicea and of 150 who later were convened at Constantinople (381). Though its precise origin is uncertain, it has carried great weight in both Eastern and Western churches. From about 500 A.D. on, it came to be used in place of the Nicene Creed.

⁷ *Encyclopadie*, 565.

⁸ Tillich, Paul. *A Reinterpretation of the Doctrine of the Incarnation*, Church Quarterly Review (1949) p. 135.

3

A Contemporary Vision of the Trinity

Belief in the Trinity has become a relic of the past, an intellectual curiosity, to many people in contemporary society. They find it difficult to follow the speculations and circumlocutions of theologians as they struggle to disentangle Biblical views from Hellenistic thought patterns, as they seek to separate metaphysical strait jackets from dynamic, Scriptural teachings about God. Speculations about the Trinity seem irrelevant to citizens struggling for survival on a planet torn by internicene brush wars, threats of nuclear holocaust, and impending famine. Even involved church people, wrapped up in fund raising drives, ecclesiastical reorganizations, social service projects and study programs, have little awareness of the significance of the Trinity for their world. Indeed, some consider the Trinity to be a hindrance blocking a synthesis of Christianity with other world religions.

On the other hand, there are those who are convinced that the Trinity is the dynamic, all powerful reality which can unify humanity and give new life to society. These believe that the church, if she catches a new, realistic vision of the Trinity and becomes truly committed to the Triune God, can lead the way toward a new world culture. Although a perfect society is impossible on a planet inhabited by imperfect humans, a nobler society than we know could be possible.

One of the basic ailments of human society is its deep seated fragmentation. Each person is surrounded by throngs of people, billions of stars, unnumbered atoms and molecules, each of which is unique and distinct. All are moving kaleidoscopically about him, confusing him and deepening the fragmentation of his experience of life.

People in every culture have sought for some great unity which can unify the diverse elements of existence. Asian culture has produced a magnificent symbol which declares the unity yet differentiation of reality. One of the oldest pieces of Chinese literature is the *I Ching* (*Book of Change*) which has been revered both by Confucianists and Taoists. The *Book of Change* describes yin and yang as the primary categories of existence. This notion which may have originated during the Han dynasty (206 B.C.–220 A.D.) views yin as the shadowy, female, passive, cold dimension side of existence and yang as the bright, male, creative, aggressive, warm side. Yin and yang cannot exist without each other. They signify the complementarity of opposites. The idea contains the western concept of becoming in that it represents motion. It also is transcendent in that it transcends rational, analytic, logical reason. It represents an ultimate unity and wholeness which contains diversity and differentiation.

Yin-yang thought embodies both/and thinking in contradistinction to much western thought which is either/or. Yet, yin-yang thinking which deals with ultimate issues contains the potential for either/or thought which deals with penultimate issues. Both/and thought has an ally in modern scientific thought which, for example, accepts both the wave and quantum theories of light. Yin and yang thought superbly represents the complementarity, the mutual dependency/independency, the unity and the differentiation which characterizes reality.

This symbol which for millenia has resided within the psyche of Chinese and Indians reflects an intuitive view of the ultimate which exists in the hearts and minds of unnumbered millions of humanity. Could it be that such a widely held view, at least in part, is an accurate perception of the unifying power of the ultimate? Could it be that the view that yin and yang belong together in one sublime unity is the highest and deepest reach of natural human intuition? Could it be that one of the noblest intuitions of Asian thought finds its highest completion not in yin-yang, but in a Trinity which is one differentiated whole? Certainly, there is a significant parallel between the Trinity properly understood and yin-yang. Both emphasize that there is both differentiation and magnificent unity at the heart of reality.

In the midst of the multitudinous fragments of reality which are incessantly whirling about and within him, western man also has sought persistently for some unity which can explain and overcome both his own inner disunity and the atomization of his experience of life. The Ionian philosophers of nature sought a common element from which all things had sprung. Thales thought it was water. Anaximenes described it as air. Anaximander saw it as an undefinable boundless. Parmenides called it being. Each was seeking one common denominator for all things. During the European Middle Ages, people saw the primordial unity in God. Isaac Newton described the cosmic unity of earthly and heavenly laws. In more recent times, a scientific culture has tended to see all things as reducible to one thing, matter. Vitalism has slowly yielded ground to a reductionistic materialism. Charles Darwin viewed natural selection as the principle which explained all things. Karl Marx described the great unifying force of life as dialectical materialism. Albert Einstein stumbled upon relativity as he sought one principle to explain and to unify all reality. Yet the unity which explains and encompasses all things has been elusive and incomprehensible.

Nevertheless, men have continued the quest. Man, the paradox of the ages, stands in a world of vast diversity, variety, fragmentation, and alienation. Yet a powerful counter force endeavors to drive things toward each other. Even the smallest and most delicate of organisms, the mitochondria (cells within cells), demonstrate a primal urge to form linkages and relationships which support all life. A centripetal power prompts all things toward interdependence and interrelatedness. Man has an inner urge to understand what may be the strongest force in the universe—a convergence of all things toward togetherness, toward unity, toward oneness.

Could it be that the unity which underlies all of reality is God? Could it be that the Divine unity is itself infinitely complex? Could it be that the Trinity, inexhaustibly rich in both unity and diversity, is the power which sustains both the infinite variety of reality and the ultimate unity of all things?

What is the Trinitarian vision which can enrich human life and can explain the unity underlying reality? That vision certainly must correspond to reality. It cannot be the fabrication of clever human minds. Man's theological speculations must be suspect if they claim to be completely accurate representations of the divine reality since finite, faulted human minds cannot penetrate the infinite source of reality. If people are to be engaged by the Infinite who underlies the reality they experience, the Infinite must disclose itself to them. Consequently, revelation, the self-disclosure of the Infinite, must be the basis of man's understanding of God. We must listen to revelation if we are to encounter ultimate reality.

For those standing in the Judeo-Christian tradition, the Infinite has intervened into finitude. God has interacted with His creation. The ultimate has disclosed itself. The transcendent has descended into human history. Biblical history claims to be an inspired account of God's self-revelation to humankind. Those who would pursue an understanding of the God called Triune must attend to that revelation with listening hearts and minds.

The God who revealed Himself to the Biblical prophets and sages is not static, subsisting being like Aristotle's Unmoved Mover. Rather, He is the personal God who is His own divine self mover. Self movement is a characteristic of His divine independence and freedom.[1] He is the sovereign Lord, totally independent and free to act as He chooses. Consequently, He is free to create, free to reveal Himself to Himself, and free to reveal Himself to His creation. God's sovereign Lordship is total freedom and untrammeled possibility, including the possibility of His own self-revelation. According to the Scriptures, God's revelations of Himself are actions in which His being and His becoming are united in the events of historical revelation. God's transcendence and being only can be understood by creatures dwelling in history as God's being becomes disclosed in history as the divine being becoming historical.[2] In this sense, the sovereign Lord of the Bible is personal being-becoming-for-others, interpreting (revealing) Himself for His creation. Moses at the burning bush, Isaiah in the temple, Jesus at His baptism, Paul in the wilderness of Arabia, John on Patmos all experienced God's being becoming historical disclosure. God's eternity, which encompasses time (chronos) was breaking into earthly time to become revelation moments, pregnant with revelatory meaning which transformed man's time (chronos) into divine time (kairos).

Since the God described in the Biblical record is the sovereign Lord, He is described as Subject, the "I" who speaks and an event results. Creation is the object of His actions. Yet in His acts of self-revelation, He who is the divine Subject humbles Himself, allowing creatures made in His own image to become subjects who can view Him as an object of their attention. God's "I", once revealed, permits human subjects to speak of "Him" and "Thou". This is part of His condescension, His humiliation, His being-as-becoming. So Moses could ask God's name (Exodus 3:13). Paul could ask "Who are you, Lord?" (Acts 9:5) By responding "I am who I am" and by saying "I am Jesus", the divine Subject subjected himself to man. By revealing Himself, the divine Subject took the humiliating risk of letting man become a subject to whom God would be the object.

Revelation, then, has become possible. The divine Lord can be known in and through His revelatory events in history. The Bible describes God's acts of self-revelation, self-disclosure, and self-interpretation. The Bible represents those revelatory events to contemporary men and women. As people read or hear of those events, time may dissolve in their minds, and they can be transported into those great revelatory moments. As they participate in the Biblical representations of God's mighty, historical acts, it is as though they were there at creation, at the Red Sea crossing, at Sinai, at Calvary, and at the empty tomb. They have the opportunity to experience God's revealings about Himself and themselves.

That revelation is necessary because finite creatures cannot grasp the infinite any more than an ant can comprehend a man towering over it. Human reason and intuition have severe limitations. They are colored by a person's prejudices, likes and dislikes, the state of one's health, the web of psychological conditioning begun in one's mother's womb and shaped by one's genetic inheritance. Reason often leads to contradictions which cannot be resolved by reason. Intuition often leads into a subjectivism which lacks correspondence with reality. Even empiricism with its emphasis on sensory data cannot be relied upon for a knowledge of infinite reality since empirical data is affected by the observer and the interpretation of empirical data must utilize conditioned reason and intuition. Moreover, transcendent reality cannot be crammed into a test tube or weighed on scales. Consequently, a finite human must look to revelation for valid knowledge of the infinite.

The Bible describes revelatory events which were experienced by a host of persons. The point of contact between the Revealer and human beings appears to be the self-transcendence of personhood. The divine Person is the divine "I" who discloses His being to the human person who is "thou". God's disclosures have been made in human history. Persons have experienced revelatory events and through those events have encountered the mediated immediacy of a divine Person (i.e. Moses at the burning bush, Isaiah in the temple, Paul on the Damascus road, John on Patmos, etc.). Out of such Person to person encounters, feelings became thoughts, which became words, which, guided by a divine Person, have accurately reflected the divine self-disclosures to humans.

Such words have been written down by the inspired authors of Holy Scripture. The sacred writings provide the data of historic revelation. Those who read or hear the revelatory data with teachable hearts and minds can be guided by the Spirit of Truth (cf. John 16:13) into an understanding of God and into participation in His divine life. The revelations of God in history become experienced and confirmed in the minds and hearts of men and women under the impact both of the Spirit and of the Scriptures.

A host of believing men and women have experienced the revelations of God. As they have probed the data of revelation

(Scriptures), as they have examined their own experiences, they have found that their experiences are of God as Father, as Son, as Spirit—Fatherly goodness, Christly redemption, and spiritual sanctification. Through the ages, the disclosures of Holy Writ have been and remain the primary data concerning God and His revelations.

Such disclosures have revealed that God is one. Through Moses the message was given: "Hear, O Israel: the Lord our God is one Lord." (Deut. 6:4) The actual Hebrew states "Yahweh, our God, Yahweh, one." That which was to be worshipped and adored by Israel was not to be a pantheon of deities, but was to be Yahweh, who is one.

The name Yahweh, used about 6700 times in the Old Testament, derived from God's disclosure to Moses at the burning bush. That sacred name by which God gave Himself to Israel through Moses was "I will be what I will be." (Exod. 3:13) A name in the ancient world represented an intimate and binding relation between it and its subject. The subject along with its nature and power was in the name. "I will be what I will be" revealed the divine, personal, self-moving, eternal Subject—"I".

Gerhard von Rad noted that "Yahweh had only one name; Marduk had fifty. . ."[3] The use of that one supreme name reflected the fact that the God of Israel was one. Israel did not add a host of other equally significant names because she viewed God as sublimely one. Although Israel called God by other names, they were not names which stood alongside or compared to Yahweh in their fullness. That exalted name was the one supreme name of the God who was one.

The first commandment, although not directly affirming the unity of God, affirmed that Yahweh was the only God in Israel. The words "I am Yahweh, your God" acknowledges a world where polytheism was widespread, although they certainly do not affirm the existence of other gods. The monotheism of Israel became more explicit in the writings of Isaiah: "I am Yahweh, besides me there is no God." (Isa. 45:5) Implicit both in the first commandment and in the prophetic writings are the convictions that the God of Israel is both the One who is ultimate and the

One whose unity is expressed by one name which is above all other names (Yahweh).

Yahweh's unity expresses itself in His unifying sovereignty over all things. The divine unity is the basis of the unity and order in nature. God's sovereignty contains the necessity of His unity. Power requires unity, and infinite power is intertwined with ultimate oneness. Fragmentation of power inevitably brings disunity just as disunity and disharmony produce a fragmentation of power. Concentration of power inevitably results in intensification of unity. In God, infinite, sovereign power is supported and accompanied by intense oneness. His sovereignty and His oneness are two facets of the same reality.

Yet God's oneness is complex and differentiated according to the Biblical revelation. Too often His unity has been considered to be a simple, mathematical oneness. Yet every unity has some complexity. One person may be a son, a father, a husband, a banker, a Mason, a Methodist, a Republican. One person may have many facets and dimensions to his personality. One stone may contain mica, granite, and a host of chemicals. One atom may contain a whole universe. Unity is complex and differentiated. The higher the level of being, the more intense and complex becomes the unity.

The Bible frequently speaks of the differentiations in God as being threefold. For example, Isaiah (61:1 ff) speaks of Yahweh, of one who is His messenger and of the Spirit abiding upon the messenger. The New Testament explicitly speaks of Father, Son, and Holy Spirit in whose name Christ's followers were to be baptized. (Matt. 28:19) Paul (Romans 1:1-4) speaks of the Author of the Gospel, the content of the Gospel (Jesus Christ) and the instrument (Holy Spirit) by whom Christ has been "designated" Son of God. In the apostolic benediction (2 Corinthians 13:13), he attributes grace to Jesus Christ, love to the Father, and fellowship to the Holy Spirit. In Ephesians, he says, "through Him (Christ) we both have access in one Spirit to the Father." (Eph. 2:18) At times in the New Testament, the words Father, Son and Spirit are used almost interchangeably as though each was a "double" of the other. For example, grace is attributed to God (Rom. 5:15), to Christ (Rom. 16:20) and to both (Rom. 1:7). Robert Jenson notes that "In Paul the standard Hebrew theological predicates take either God or Jesus as subject, or both at once."[4]

The Old Testament, although containing intimations of a plurality in God (cf. Genesis 1:26), emphasized the oneness of God. Yet a pure, simple undifferentiated unity in God would be in stark contrast to a differentiated, empirical world. It cannot explain motion and may deny movement, or worse, it may deny the world. It cannot be loving or holy or free in its essential nature since love requires an eternal beloved, since holiness requires distinction and differentiation, and since freedom requires someone or something with which one can identify.

The New Testament maintains belief in the unity of God, but also delineates a plurality in oneness. Father, Son, and Holy Spirit are God. Each is intimately related to the Godhead. Each fulfills, not limits, the others. Each is personal and much more. Different understandings of their relationship have emerged among believers throughout the centuries. Subordinationism appeared and reappeared. Christ and the Spirit were understood by some to be inferior to the Father. Yet the New Testament pictures them as equal. (Matt. 28:19) Modalism also has reoccurred, even in the 20th century. Modalism, like subordinationism, veils the God behind Father, Son, and Holy Spirit so that it is difficult, if not impossible, to comprehend the God who is ultimate. By isolating an unnameable and indefinable ultimate behind the three, modalists not only imply that a fourth reality (i.e. substance) is really god, but also make it well nigh impossible to speak of His having any history since that reality or substance is changeless.

The Bible, however, depicts the one, true God as love. (I John 4:8,16) As love, God is conscious and personal since love can exist only for a conscious, personal self. Augustine was correct in saying that God is His attributes, God *is* His own love personified. God's love is His being-in-action, His being for others. God's love eternally unifies Him and focuses His power.

Yet love is complex and differentiated. Self-giving love can exist only in the presence of some other to love.

The unchanging God is love, was love in eternity past, will be love in eternity future. Prior to creation, the one, great God loved. Yet, before the creation of all that is, who or what did He love? Since His nature is eternal love, there must have been another uncreated One to love. Since God is love, He would have ceased to exist if there were none other to love. A God who is love must be eternally related. Love cannot survive apart from relationship. Love demands an Other.

The Biblical record teaches that within the unity of God there eternally have existed three Lovers. Their love is not a separate reality. It is one personality reaching out to another personality in a special relationship. The Father loves and is loved by His Son. (John 17:24) Father and Son love and are loved by the Spirit. Love exists because there is a plurality in the one great God.

Love requires one conscious self to give love freely and another conscious self to receive love freely. Love, to be love, requires freedom to love. Yet, the loved self must have some likeness to the loving self. Jurgen Moltmann has put it that love in the Triune God is not addressed "to the Other in the like, but to the like in the Other."[5] There must be some similarity to serve as a point of contact. Persons who love each other deeply must share, at least, conscious, self-transcending personhood. The depth of love will depend upon the similarity of their interests and characteristics. In God the selves who love each other eternally are like each other in many ways but particularly in that they are selves with a conscious identity. The intensity and richness of their love is related to the intense similarity of their interests and natures. Indeed, each according to Scripture is the alter ego of the others. Love, therefore, requires both a differentiation of identities (persons) as well as an intense likeness and unity in God.

What is meant when believers have described God as persons who love? They are reflecting Biblical teaching which uses personal pronouns and verbs to describe God. The God of the

Bible loves, thinks, and interacts with human persons. But the finite, when seeking to speak of the Infinite, must recognize the infinite gulf separating a human person from a divine person. Negatively, a divine person is vastly different from a human, qualitatively and quantitatively, in power, intelligence, consciousness, and other capabilities. Positively, there also are similarities between a human and a divine person. Both love, think, and will, but in significantly different ways and capacities. That is why humans have been viewed by Biblical writers as being in the image of God. God in condescending to reveal Himself to man has focused infinite personhood upon human personhood. The divine persons, unlike human persons, have a fulness of personality which is incapable of any enrichment. They not only have personhood, they are the source of all personhood.

In the last analysis, man is unable to define divine personhood beyond saying that it is vastly different but somewhat like human personhood. The Sabellian modalists first applied the word persona or mask to the Trinity who, for them, was one god behind three masks or appearances. The Greek theologians, however, used the word hypostases to speak of the individual existences of the Father, Son, and Spirit. Hypostases had a deeper ontological significance. The Latin theologians preferred to retain the use of the word person though, for them, it came to mean the unique identity of an individual existent. Boethius and the Council of Florence defined a divine person as "an individual substance of a rational nature." Many later theologians seemed to prefer this rather than Aquinas' definition of a person as "a distinct subsistent in an intellectual nature." In modern times, some have tended to view a person as a center of consciousness which not only has existence but also acts as an existing self.[6] Karl Rahner, however, has pointed out that considering the three persons of the Trinity merely as three centers of consciousness could lead to a tritheism.[7]

Augustine's understanding still seems to be in accord with Biblical representations. The three divine persons or hypostases share one rational nature but in different ways—as Father, as

Son, as Holy Spirit. The inner being of God (Father, Son, Spirit) is eternally shaped by the eternal relations each has with the others. Each divine person is a rational, loving, willing individual who possesses with the others an intellectual nature which enables each to know and to relate to the others. Each person acts according to His unique nature and mission. Each person is a center for the other persons. Unlike human relationships which occur on the edge of a person's ego, the interaction of the divine persons occurs at the center of each divine self. Each is the alter ego of the others. Each is the central focus of the others' being.

The three loving selves who together are the one great, self-sufficient God are interdependent. Love nourishes a deep interrelatedness and oneness at the core of their beings. Their love begets the unity which focuses their sovereign power. Each individual person freely chooses to interrelate and to depend on the others.

God knows Himself as Father as He knows and loves Himself in relation to the Son and Spirit. The Son and Spirit know the Father, themselves, and each other as they draw their life from the Father and from each other. The Son knows Himself as Son by His relation to the Father. The Spirit knows Himself as the Spirit of God or as the Spirit of Christ as He experiences Himself in His unique relationship to Father and Son. Though their relationships individuate and differentiate them, their relations do not constitute their differences. Their relationships manifest their distinctions.

Although the three separate identities in the one God choose to be eternally interrelated and interdependent, none creates another. The Father does not create the self of the Son although He may eternally bestow Sonship upon Him. The three selves eternally coexist and cohere as one in the intensity of an eternal, unifying love which is the nature of each. Yet, that love has no independent existence. It is the manifestation of the nature of the three as they relate to each other. Each exists eternally as an individual self or hypostasis. The three are interdependent, for the Father is not Father apart from His relationship of Father to the Son. The Son is not the Son apart from His relation to His

Father. The Spirit is not the Spirit of the Father or of the Son apart from His relation to those who constitute the Godhead with Him. Each eternally depends upon the others.

They are not only interdependent, but also influence and permeate one another in love. (John 14:10, 17:21) The three eternal identities, described in the Biblical revelation as one, interpenetrate each other with perfect empathy, with a perfect blending of being, thought, desire, and will. Three individual selves blend into one consciousness in loving each other. The teaching of perichoresis, first applied to theology by John of Damascus, expressed the conviction that the three in one God passed over into one another so that the Father was in the Son and Spirit even as they were in Him. Fathers of the Latin Church spoke of each dwelling in the other and of all three permeating each other. This did not minimize the teaching that each was separate and different from the other. Rather, it underscored the oneness of the three in eternal love. It also underscored the perfect equality of the three and eliminated any hint of subordinationism.

Both the Bible and church tradition present the three in one as each having a different and unique function. The Father begets. The Son is the only begotten. The Holy Spirit is the sent One or the One who proceeds. In the context of divine love, to beget means to bring forth, to pour one's life into another, to be a channel of life, nourishment, and direction to another as well as to receive love, obedience and honor from the begotten. In the context of love, to be begotten is to receive, to receive life so that one may pass on life, to be the image of the Giver, to communicate in love with the Giver, to accomplish the will of the Giver, to be nourished by the Giver so that the One receiving may nourish others. In the framework of divine love, to be the One sent (the Spirit) is to receive an identity and a mission by virtue of One's relation to the Sender. The Sent also is to draw on the resources of the Sender, to be one with the purposes of the Sender, to communicate in love with the Sender, to accomplish the will of the Sender, and to return to the Sender. Historically, the Church has understood the Father God to be the begetter, the source of life, love, and power, God the Son to be the only begotten of the Father who is the image of the invisible God, and God the Spirit to be the One sent to do God's will. In the love each has for the other the Father (Giver and Sender), the Son (Receiver and Image), and the Spirit (Sent and Returnee) are three "I"'s who are "we".

According to Karl Barth's interpretation of Scripture, they also are Revealer (Father, Giver), Revelation (Son, Receiver), Revealedness (Spirit, Sent). Self-giving love, by nature, must share. The veiled, but eternal Revealer (Father, Giver) opens Himself to share with the Son and Spirit. In that sharing, the Revealer knows Himself as the eternal Father. The eternal Revelation (Son, Receiver) unveils or opens Himself to receive, to share, and to show forth the divine wonders and glories. As He receives and shares the Father's glory, He eternally knows Himself as the Son. The eternal Revealedness (Spirit, Sent) eternally opens Himself to receive, to impart, and to share that Revelation, as well as to effect God's purposes and to glorify God forever. In the process of sharing the glory of God, He eternally knows Himself as the Spirit of God. As each shares with the Others in love, each also knows both Himself and the Others. Each through His relation to the others eternally knows Himself vis a vis the Others.

Tragically, the church was sundered in 1054 A.D. because the western church formally adopted the phrase "filioque". The western church, having inserted "filioque" into the Niceno-Constantinopolitan creed, held that the Holy Spirit proceeded from the Father *and* the Son. The eastern church held that the Spirit proceeded only from the Father. The Father according to Scripture is the Source of the Holy Spirit who proceeds from Him. (John 15:26) Yet, as Bolotov and Moltmann have pointed out, the Father is the Father of the Son, therefore, the Son is intimately related to the One from whom the Spirit proceeds. Moreover, the Spirit is sent through the Son to glorify the Son. Therefore, both the eastern and western churches, although using somewhat different terminology, were describing the same reality from slightly different perspectives. Each emphasized a facet of the truth. The Spirit proceeds from the Father, but because of the perichoresis and the intimate relation of Father and Son, it is not amiss to say He proceeds from the Father and the Son.[8]

The long history of the discussions about procession may seem irrelevant to many Christians. Yet, their significance lies in man's effort to understand the relations of the three persons. Most of the interminable discussions have been man's attempt to build mental constructs which express the deeper relation among the three persons. Theologians generally have followed Aquinas' teaching that the Son proceeds from the Father by intellect and the Spirit proceeds by the will. They also have believed that the Father generates the procession of the Son while the Spirit is not generated but simply proceeds or is breathed forth (spiration) from the Father and the Son. As the Son is generated eternally by the Father, the Father's person and character are reproduced in the Son so that "He is the image of the invisible God." (Col. 1:15) As the Spirit proceeds from the Father and Son, their love and life are impressed upon the Spirit. As the Spirit returns His love to the Son and the Father, His love and personhood are reflected in their persons.

Since God is self-giving love, He experiences the pain and suffering caused by the rejection of the creation He loves. God is a perfectly harmonious Spirit who experiences a non-physical personal and spiritual pain which originates from beyond the self. Just as God's love requires another to love—so His pain requires the existence of others since pain, at least initially, is a response of the self to something which is not the self. Despite the Greek notion of the divine incapacity for suffering (apathy), the heartaches of God, as His covenants were broken and as His Christ suffered, force us to realize that the eternal God of self-giving love suffers. The drama of God's infinite sorrow only is possible in a differentiated God. The most intense pain arises when one beholds his most beloved suffering. Infinite pain pierced God the Father when His Son was in agony. Infinite pain crushed the Son as He saw His Father reviled. Infinite pain grieves the Spirit when men reject the Father and Son. Triunity in God provides the only adequate explanation of the depth of the sufferings of the Infinite God. The intense love within the Trinity is the ground of the love shed outward by the Triune God. It also is the basis of God's infinite pain when He later is confronted by an unloving creation which rejects Him in His Son and Spirit.

The divine experience of pain necessitates differentiation in God. The Greeks were correct when they insisted that undifferentiated, transcendent being is beyond the reach of suffering (apathy). A solitary infinite cannot be gripped by pain since it is infinitely above and beyond that which causes pain. Without the differentiations in God described by the Bible, without the descent of the Spirit to brood over creation and to search the hearts of people, without the Incarnation of God the Son when He stooped to identify with rebellious humanity, God would exist in aloof, untouched isolation. Pain in a God of Infinite Power requires a love which can be touched by rejection. Love requires a Lover (the Father), a Beloved (the Son), and Love which is communicated (the Spirit). Pain in God presupposes love which requires a plurality in God. Without the Triune God in the shadows surrounding the cross, the pains of the Son of God have no ultimate meaning, no unique significance. For the painful cross to have eternal significance, there must be a trinity in God.

Whether or not God suffered before creation, we cannot know. We only can speculate. In the dim recesses of eternity, according to the Bible, "God created the heavens and the earth." (Gen. 1:1) That which was formless (chaos) may have been a source of pain and suffering to God at creation. What is certain is that from the instant anything that was not God was given being and existence, God was confronted with an other than God. Creation was divine self-humiliation as the self-sufficient, self-contained God enabled created things to share His reality. As Jurgen Moltmann has pointed out in his discussion of Isaac Luria's doctrine of Zimsum, God limited Himself in the act of creation. Luria dealt with the question of how the omnipresent God who is "all in all" can allow anything that is not God to exist. He suggested that the "existence of the universe was made possible through a shrinkage process in God" which made room for creation.⁹

Right from the instant that anything which was not God was created, the possibility of pain in God became real. That pain has been seen in the sorrow of the Father, the agonies of the Son, and the grieving of the Spirit.

In infinite freedom and love, the Father God created all that is *for* the Son whom He loves eternally. (Col. 1:16) He also created *through* the Son (John 1:3,10) and *by* the operation of the Spirit. He created humans for fellowship with the Son and for communion with the Spirit. But He offers them freedom to respond to that promise of fellowship. Yet man has rejected God, has rebelled (Genesis 3) and has plunged creation into a state where it is out of harmony with God's purposes. This has caused a holy God infinite pain. Some like Kazo Kitamori, the Japanese theologian, see the pain of God resulting from the tension in God between His love and His wrath (holiness) in the face of human sin.¹⁰ At this point, it is important to note that the God of the Bible experiences pain but is not pain. He experiences pain in dealing with creation, but at the end there will be an end to all pain. (Rev. 21:4) To set things right the eternal Son of God has entered into the human drama to become God in human flesh. The incarnate God became one with humanity in order to redeem humanity. In a sense, the Incarnation, as Moltmann has said, "intervenes in the inner relations of the Trinity."¹¹ The holy God empties, limits, and painfully humiliates Himself to give humans opportunity to see and to respond to His love. The result is the crucifixion of the God-man. At the cross God was sublimely being-in-becoming. Jesus, writhing in agony on the cross, not only suffered pain at the hands of sinful men, not only revealed the suffering a holy God has known as His creation resists and rebels against Him, but also is love in action. There He unveiled the pain which human sin has brought the Triune God. As Christ absorbed the sins of the world on Calvary, the holy Father turned His face away from the Son. "God is forsaken by God."¹² The Triune relationship of love was ruptured and infinite pain stabbed both Son and Father. The stab into Jesus' side also was a stab into the heart of the Father. Such infinite pain only is understandable if there is a true differentiation of loving persons in God. Only if the Infinite Father is pained by the agony of His Infinite Son and by the grieving of His Infinite Spirit can the Infinite experience infinite pain.

At the same time, the Incarnation and crucifixion reveal not only the pain of love but also the intense love of the Son for the Father which was demonstrated by the Son's loving obedience to His Father's will. That love increases as each fallen person responds in love to the divine love revealed in the cross and resurrection and spread into human hearts by the Spirit. A reborn humanity comes to participate in the many-splendored love binding the Father, Son, and Spirit. So the Spirit is sent upon all flesh and the glorification of the Father and Son spreads from life to life throughout the earth. The power driving the redemptive wave sweeping the earth is divine love. Love for the Father and for a lost humanity caused the Son to endure the pain of the cross. Love for the Father and Son as well as for a rebellious creation sent the Spirit to strive painfully with human hearts and wills. Love for the Father, Son, and Spirit is welling up within millions of human spirits who have responded to that love. That love has known pain. That love has been spit upon, has been scourged, has known bitter rejection, has been crucified in the process of producing an increase of love in the universe. That love inhabiting believers has known persecution, torture, and rejection, yet, has brought about a great ground swell of love upon the earth. The flow of love earthward has been from the Father, through the Son, by the Spirit. The resulting tide of love heavenward has been from the Spirit, through the Son to the Father. Love from God the Father and through God the Son and by God the Spirit has resulted in love from God the Spirit working in human spirits ascending heavenward through God the Son at the right hand of Power to God the Father upon the throne of the universe. Love in, through, and by the Triune God is the all in all of redemption. Yet, that love which has borne infinite suffering and pain has multiplied love.

A Contemporary Vision of the Trinity

If what has been said is a fair representation of the Triune God, how can we summarize the vision of the Trinity? God is the unity which overshadows and saturates all reality with His harmonizing presence. His transcendence is His absolute freedom to actualize unlimited possibilities. God is not a substance nor impersonal being. Rather, God is suprapersonality with infinite love and power undergirding, pervading, and unifying all that is. In the one great God, there are three eternal identities each of whom is infinitely beyond personhood as we know personhood. Each is personal, but infinitely more than personal. Each encompasses and includes the noblest characteristics of male and female life.[13] Each is a rational, conscious identity and more. There is the Father who fathers all that is. There is the Son who makes visible the Father's love and power. There is the Spirit who radiates the power and glory of the Father and Son throughout all reality. The three love each other so intensely that they are bound together in an eternal and indissoluble oneness. Each one's consciousness interpenetrates the consciousness of the others to become a common consciousness. Their love one for the other is infinitely beyond love as persons can conceive it. In that love the personality of each flows into the others. Their oneness in love coalesces their thoughts, wills, feelings, consciousness, and power into perfect harmony. Their mutual love is the perfect community for which all people yearn. They are the sublime community which is the model for human society. Their unity is expressed as their love, sovereignty, and complementarity. Their perfect unity is the source, the telos and the eschaton (end) of all that is. To participate in their life is salvation. To share in their love is perfect health and wholeness. To be one with them is to experience their eternal life in the here and now. God, viewed internally, is one. God turning inward to express love among His three persons is perfect unity. God viewed in His outward relations with creation is sovereign and three. These two perspectives unite in a complementary manner whenever a person experiences a living faith in the divine three-in-one.

How is such a faith relationship with the Triune God brought about? How does a human enter into union with the Divine? Usually one first meets God amidst painful darkness. Then the divine love is revealed out of darkness. Then a relationship of love between a human and the holy Trinity elevates a human being to participate in the feelings, thoughts, and life of God. God offers love to all people, but humans are alienated from God. Rebellion and sin have separated them from Him. When a person is given a knowledge of Christ, humbles himself in repentance, and asks forgiveness from the Crucified, the barrier between God and man dissolves. Through a knowledge of the Son of God and by the willing love of the Spirit of God, God and man enter into a person to Person relation. A person then is able to participate in God's life and the process of man's divinization is under way. The breakthrough from darkness into light occurs between man and the Son of God. Man through Christ (the Revelation) is put in touch both with the Father (the Revealer) and with the Holy Spirit (the Revealedness) He experiences the power of the love that each of the divine persons has for the others and responds by loving God and by giving himself to other humans who are loved by God. He becomes part of an earthly community modeled after the Triune community. He tastes of the divine holiness, righteousness, wisdom, and power. He becomes fully human in God. He rises from a subhuman existence to the fully human existence God planned when He created humanity. Man becomes godlike as he more and more participates in the life of God through prayer, immersion in the Sacred Scriptures, and in holy, just living which expresses God's love. As his life flows more and more into the Triune God, he finds himself also pouring his life out into the life of the world. He finds himself thinking theologically within the ultimate paradigm which is the Trinity.

People, as they participate in the life of the Trinity, also grow in God by faith. Faith is a gift from God. It unites the visions of God's oneness and threeness. Real faith participates in the faith God has in Himself. The three persons of the Trinity have infinite faith both in themselves and in each other. Men and women in God share in God's unshakeable and infinite certitude about Himself.

They also are filled with hope. Though the eternal Trinity encompasses all time in His eternal "nowness," what Christians view as the future is God's creativity eternally bringing forth that which is new. Creativity, like love and pain, also requires a plurality in God since to create what is not God, God must be a plurality which enables Him to go beyond Himself. The Bible depicts God as having come to humanity in the past, as being with us in the present and as coming to us from the future (from creative newness). Christ will come a second time in the future. Judgment and the perfect community of the eternal Kingdom are waiting in the future. With each new sunrise, God comes in new ways. As people in God anticipate God's creative newness in each new dawning, they are filled with the hope, certitude, and optimism about the future which is in the Triune God Himself. The Trinity opens man's future to the infinite possibilities of the Infinite God.

Humanity can be both humanized and divinized by participation in the life of the Trinity. Humanity can rise to new levels of existence in God. Humanity, sharing in the life of God, can be divinized, can become fully human or god-like. A divinized humanity can bring forth a new Trinitarian community upon planet Earth.

NOTES

[1] Cf. Jungel, Eberhard, *The Doctrine of the Trinity*, (Grand Rapids: Eerdmans, 1976), p. 93.

[2] Ibid., p.94.

[3] von Rad, Gerhard, *Old Testament Theology*, (New York: Harper and Row, 1962), v. 1, p. 185.

[4] Jenson, Robert W., *The Triune Identity*, (Philadelphia: Fortress Press, 1982), p.41.

[5] Moltmann, Jurgen, *The Trinity and the Kingdom*, (San Francisco: Harper and Row, 1981), p.59.

[6] Cf. Dewart, Leslie, *The Future of Belief*, (New York: Herder and Herder, 1966), p. 147.

[7] Rahner, Karl, *The Trinity*, (New York: Herder & Herder, 1970), pp.

106–109. Joseph Bracken points out that the three separate persons "together form a single shared consciousness . . . which thus corresponds exactly to their communitarian reality as one God." Bracken, Joseph, *The Triune Symbol*, (Lanham, MD, University Press of America, 1985), p.25.

[8] Moltmann, Op. Cit., pp. 179–180.

[9] Ibid. p.109.

[10] Choan-Seng Song, *Third Eye Theology*, (Maryknoll, New York: Orbis Books, 1979), p. 60.

[11] Op. cit., p.119.

[12] Moltmann, J., Op. cit., p.80.

[13] This volume purposely does not deal with the gender of God because such discussions tend to view the transcendent God as more human than divine and because it seems obvious that the God who created and undergirds all things encompasses both male and female characteristics. (Cf. Isa. 66:13; Ps. 131:2; 17:8; 36:7; Deut. 32:11,12; Luke 15:8–10, etc.) Since both man and woman were created in the image of God, God contains both male and female qualities on a cosmic scale. Yet such an acknowledgement should not be interpreted as justification for denying that God is Father, Son, and Holy Spirit. That would destroy the heart of Christianity. cf. Bloesch, Donald, *The Battle for the Trinity*, (Ann Arbor, Servant Publications, 1985.)

4

Certainty About The Triune God

In a secular age, a question which must be addressed is whether or not the church's understanding of the Trinity corresponds with reality. Is God actually Triune? Does the Triune God really exist? Is our finite description of the infinite God an accurate representation of reality? Can we be certain of the Trinity?

It must be acknowledged, of course, that the frail words of finite humans never can contain or adequately describe the Infinite. Yet, Christians who believe that God has revealed something of Himself in nature, in history, and by the Scriptures also assume that the words and statements of Scripture are capable of analogically mirroring something of His self revelation. Since Scripture for most Christians is considered authoritative in its revelation of the ultimately real, they regard it as reliable when it speaks of God as Father, Son, and Holy Spirit. Consequently, the Christian's beliefs and actions grow out of the twin assumptions that God has revealed Himself through Sacred Scripture and that He is Triune. The Triune God is the source of Scripture, while Scripture is the means of knowing Him as Triune. This is validated in Christian experience because the Scripture is self authenticating. The Spirit who inspired its words (I Cor 2:13) authenticates them in the psyche of believers. "The sheep follow Him for they know His voice." (John 10:4) So the person of faith who probes the data of revelation (Sacred Scripture) becomes assured that the one great God is Father, Son, and Holy Spirit though such words only faintly reflect His grandeur.

Proceeding on the faith assumptions that there is a God (1)

who has revealed Himself both in history and in Sacred Scripture and (2) that He is Triune, Christians are able to compare the adequacy of their faith assumptions with the faith assumptions of their atheist, humanist, Marxist, and other non-Christian neighbors. Everyone lives by faith assumptions whether or not he realizes it. Without some key assumptions, humans would be totally incapable of linking together the multitudinous data of life into meaningful patterns. Everyone lives by primary presuppositions or principles which are determinative for his attitudes, beliefs, and actions in life. One may or may not be aware of his first principles, but without basic principles or assumptions, one is unable to connect the raw data of experience into patterns of meaning. Without some key, some interpretive principle, people would be forced into total skepticism and would be unable even to speak intelligently.

Since everyone lives by some faith principle, the Christian can evaluate his along with those of others. Such evaluations may not be necessary for the believer who joyously is participating in the life of the Trinity, but they are necessary to demonstrate the truth to an unbelieving world. Such comparisons can demonstrate the superior reasonableness and truth character of Christianity.

To evaluate various faith assumptions involves human reason. Reason should be understood not merely in its logical, discursive sense, but also in the deeper sense of the desires of the heart which direct reasoning. Reason, by itself, has not the capacity to make absolute judgments since besides being affected by desires, it is profoundly influenced both by psychological conditioning and by the known and unknown assumptions of the reasoning person.

It also must be recognized that reasoning about the ultimate has other limitations. Reasoning involves words and concepts which, being finite, cannot be univocal (terms with a single meaning both in time and eternity). If reality has a basic unity, neither can human words and concepts be completely discontinuous or equivocal (terms with different meanings in time and eternity). Instead, reasoning about the ultimate must be analogical, using terms which may mean something similar and something different. For example, in the Judeo-Christian tradition, God is both like and different from man. Similarly, God's Fatherhood and human fatherhood are analogical (similar but different). The finite words and concepts of reasoning people about the God who unifies reality must be analogical, recognizing both similarities and distinctions between time and eternity. All valid reasoning about the Triune God is basically symbolic and analogical.

This means that our language about God, though starting from the data of divine revelation, is limited because it is finite. It may mirror some of the truth about God, but it still is only a reflection of Him. Reasoning from divine revelation, we may say what God is not, we may say what God is like, but never what God actually is. Therefore, in our halting efforts to speak of the Triune God, we must do it humbly, always deferring to the clear teaching of Scripture and always treating any speculations that go beyond Scripture with tentativeness.

Yet reason, properly utilized can assist us in evaluating the various perspectives and beliefs of humanity. Built into the human mind is an awareness that a thing cannot be and not be at the same time and at the same place. An awareness of the law of noncontradiction seems to exist to some degree in all sane minds. Whether it exists as a result of conditioning or whether it is a part of the structure of the human mind, the fact is that it profoundly affects human thought and becomes at least a part of everyone's judgment about the truth or falsity of statements. It should not be absolutized, but it can be applied to people's experience of reality. Everyone uses it to judge that day has come when night passes. The day cannot be night at the same time in the same place.

As rational persons consider the faith assumptions of various world views, they invariably use reason to evaluate them. Reason will rely heavily on the primal law of non-contradiction which is engrained in human thought. Therefore, reason will endeavor to assess the various faith assumptions in light of whether or not they contradict other accepted facts of reality. This is the first criterion or test of truth.

All people have in common the facts of birth and death, sunrise and sunset, hunger and disease though their interpretations may differ widely. Do Christian presuppositions contradict the facts of human existence? Do they account for, explain, and enrich human understandings of the cosmos, of health and disease, of goodness and evil, of anguish and joy, of bondage and freedom; or do they contradict accepted facts of human experience? Though such assessments must involve a degree of subjectivity, the adequacy or inadequacy of the various faith assumptions held by humankind will become apparent as they are evaluated in light of the facts of existence.

A second criterion for the evaluation of the truth quality of different faith assumptions is whether or not they cohere or reasonably fit together. Do Christian faith assumptions fit into and complement each other, or are they inconsistent with each other? Do Christian assumptions cohere, or fit together, logically, rationally, and intuitively? How do they compare with the coherence, or lack of it, of other faith assumptions?

A third evaluation of faith assumptions is whether or not they make a difference. If belief in the Triune God is based on reality, participation in the all powerful, incredibly dynamic God should produce a new dynamic on the human scene.

Though none of these criteria, by itself, provides absolute verification of the reality of the Triune God, taken together they are able to provide such a degree of probability that they can cause an unbelieving world to consider seriously the claims of the Triune God.

Returning to the first criterion of truth, do the twin Christian assumptions that God has revealed himself in the Bible and that He is Triune contradict the facts of existence? The facts of life with which every person must deal are empirical, historical, and/or psychological. There are no known scientific "facts" which definitively repudiate or contradict either the assumption that God has revealed Himself in history and the Bible or the assumption that revelation shows God to be Triune. Science deals with the natural order. Legitimate science probes to understand how nature works. The Scriptures, using majestic symbols and analogies, assert that God is the Creator, Sustainer, and sovereign Lord of all creation, but leave to science the task of discovering *how* God's universe functions. True science, consequently, should not abandon its proper role of describing how things work in a vain endeavor to judge Christianity's claims to be a revelation of the Triune God. Science and Christianity have complementary, but distinct, roles. Neither can legitimately intrude upon the other.

Nevertheless, the question persists, are there empirical facts in the natural order which would repudiate the revelation of the Triune God? The concept of a closed natural order which makes no room for such a revelation is a philosophic notion which is an interpretation of data, but it is not the data themselves. Apart from such interpretations, to date, science has discovered no facts which disprove revelation. However, if such facts ever were discovered, facts by themselves could not disprove His existence until the whole universe could be examined. There is an element of truth in the oft repeated statement that it is impossible to disprove the existence of God until one is able to be everywhere in the universe at the same time to verify that God is not somewhere beyond human presence in the vastness of reality. Denial of a God in one place, or one culture, or one decade, or even in one solar system does not disprove the possibility of His existence in other places, cultures, decades, or solar systems, particularly since He is both hidden and revealed. So, even if some facts ever did emerge in one location to indicate the non-existence of God, it still would be impossible to say that He does not exist somewhere. We must always be wary of universal, negative judgments, but again, it must be emphasized that to date no hard facts have emerged to disprove His existence. To the contrary, the assumption that God exists accounts for the existence of the physical universe in a way that is reasonable for millions of intelligent people. Without such an assumption, science has no explanation for the first cause of all things.

Then has history produced hard facts which disprove the revelation of the Triune God? History also is composed both of facts and interpretations of facts. Interpretations of historical data necessarily are influenced by the presuppositions and prejudices of historians. Historical facts also are difficult to identify and to separate from interpretations. Though numerous interpretations of historical data deny the existence of God (i.e. Marxism), no unambiguous facts of history can disprove God's existence. On the other hand, many millions of historical personages have based their lives and actions on belief in the existence of the Triune God. They and their deeds are facts which could be adduced to support the actual existence of God.

A study of man, his psychological drives and motivations, also encompasses both facts and interpretations. Exploration into the human psyche and into the facts of human existence tend to support belief in God's reality since almost universally, people have believed in an ultimate which masses of people have called God. Contrariwise, there are no known facts which can disprove His reality though suffering, pain, and evil raise difficult questions about both His character and His existence. But apart from interpretations concerning man's nature and psychological makeup, there are no human facts to disprove the Triune God's existence. To the contrary, the facts of man's self-transcendence, of his universal search for an ultimate, of his widespread urge to pray, of his persistent belief in immortality, of his quest for goodness all point to the existence of God. The effects of the Triune God's working in the human psyche are facts which increase the probability that He exists.

It must be admitted that though there are no known facts which disprove the existence of a God who reveals Himself as Triune neither are there facts which unambiguously prove His existence. Indeed, many believers readily acknowledge His hiddenness. The Sacred Scriptures present facts which state but do not attempt to prove His existence. The question, therefore, becomes which of the many interpretations of factual data provides the most reasonable probability that He exists or does not exist.

Obviously, the committed Marxist believes that his interpretation of the facts is most probable just as the committed Christian believes that his is most probable. Each is convinced because at some point, he has become committed and commitment can produce certitude. But what of the open-minded and uncommitted person?

The one who is uncommitted but open to a commitment to something other than himself needs to see a reasonable probability which may lead him toward commitment. Since he cannot ascertain all the facts of science, history, or of human psychology, he must weigh the interpretations of real data to see which most adequately encompasses and fits the facts which he knows.

There is neither time nor space here to deal fully with this topic. Unnumbered Christians, however, have been satisfied that the Triune God who encompasses, permeates, supports and gives meaning to all the facts of reality provides the most comprehensive and satisfactory explanation of all facts. No facts are unaccounted for in His majestic plan. No facts contradict His existence. Other world views have unexplained facts. Other world views cannot account for the facts which will come to us out of the future. Other world views leave large gaps where important facts of human existence are ignored. (i.e. Confucianism's silence re. death and immortality)

Idealist philosophies generally fail to account adequately for the very real and factual human experience of physical nature. Naturalistic philosophies, including Marxism and reductionistic empiricism, fail to account for the fact that humans experience transcendence. Only Christianity with its revelation of the Triune God explains and relates in a meaningful way the data of human experience concerning both the empirical and the transcendent. For millions the adequacy and comprehensiveness of belief in the Triune God to explain all the facts of human existence provides the most satisfying and the most reasonable probability, but this, by itself, still is not compelling.

A second test of truth which may increase or decrease the probability of a world view's being true is its sense of coherence and logical consistency. Does the teaching of the Triune God fit or cohere with the rest of Christian teaching, or does it contradict any essential part of a Christian world view? Since the Triune God described in the Sacred Scriptures undergirds and encompasses all of reality, nothing is beyond His reach. All things in a Christian world view depend upon the Triune God. All things cohere in that all important doctrine. There is a magnificent coherence and dependence of all Christian doctrine upon the Triunity of God. None of the other world views can claim such superb coherence as is centered about the Triune God.

A third test of truth is whether or not it makes a difference. This is akin to the pragmatic test which evaluates truth claims against the question of their effects, particularly in and upon those who espouse the truth. Belief in the Triune God has had a massive impact upon humanity. Belief in a God of three persons has had a humanizing effect upon unnumbered multitudes, releasing a tidal wave of compassion and goodness which has expressed itself in many forms of humanitarian efforts including hospitals, schools, anti-slavery movements, and civil rights campaigns.

The divinizing effect of belief in the Trinity has lifted millions of people out of the brutishness of the sub-human toward a Christly humanity. Christians ever since Pentecost have to some degree participated in the life of the Triune God. The Apostle John quoted Jesus as praying, ". . . thou Father art in me and I in Thee, that they (His followers) also may be in us." (John 17:21) Paul put it: "I have been crucified with Christ; it is no longer I who live, but Christ who lives in me; and the life I now live in the flesh, I live by faith in the Son of God. . ." (Gal. 2:20) Peter spoke of Christ's people becoming "partakers of the divine nature." (2 Peter 1:4) Athanasius summed it up, "God became man that man might become like God." When people through faith encounter both God in Christ and God the Spirit, the Father God enters their lives and they enter into God. A mutual intermingling of the divine and human lives commences. Man participates in the life of God and is divinized in the process. "To all who received Him, who believed in his name, He gave power to become children of God." (John 1:12) Through faith, prayer, holy living, and by hearkening to God's Word, the believer shares in the love with which God loves Himself. He shares in the wisdom and joy which is shared by the persons of the Trinity. He grows into Christ-likeness of character.

For nearly two millenia, a vast host of humans have had their lives shaped and directed by the impulses of the Triune God. Such people have influenced the world on a massive scale. They have given birth to free societies. They have challenged evil and promoted goodness on a global scale. The impact of the Triune God upon believers and through them upon human affairs has been immeasurable.

Taken together, the criteria for evaluating the truth of the Trinity (its consistency with the facts of reality, its coherence with other Christian beliefs, and its effects) provide a very high degree of probability that the Trinity exists. That probability becomes certainty, however, only as rational probabilities converge in the human heart to be transformed into certainty by an actual personal experience of the persons of the Trinity.

The heart is the center of human personality. It undergirds and encompasses the thought, feelings, and will of humans. In the heart, the core of a person's being, the probabilities of the Trinity's existence are converted into certainty by divine grace.

In the 19th century, Cardinal Newman spoke of the "illative sense" which is similar to our understanding of the heart. He held that "convergent probabilities" unite in the "illative sense" to become certainty.

Earlier Pascal saw the evidences of Scripture, the church, and reason uniting in the human heart to become deep inner assurance of Christian truth. For Pascal the heart had a creative capacity to apprehend truth by uniting probabilities into certainty under the catalytic impact of divine grace. The Apostle Paul pointed to this experience of inner assurance when he spoke of the Spirit's bearing witness with our spirits. (Romans 8:16) A confirmation of the Trinity's reality ultimately is given by a personal experience of Father, Son, and Holy Spirit. Apart from that existential experience, we are left only with probabilities, albeit with strong probabilities. Apart from commitment to the strong probabilities to which reason points, there is no faith. But whenever probabilities point a seeker toward God, and whenever the Triune God Himself meets the seeker within his heart, probabilities are transformed into a certainty which is akin to the certainty which God has of His own reality. From that moment on, the seeker becomes a believer and is given profound assurance that the Triune God is real to the nth degree. After receiving such an experience of certitude, even the certitude with which God is certain of Himself, the Christian is called to relate the sovereignty of the Triune God to all of life.

5

The Trinity and Culture

Talk of the Triune God often seems abstruse, overly theological, and sometimes incomprehensible to modern men and women who are conditioned to think empirically and scientifically. How can the Trinity become meaningful to people accustomed to thinking one dimensionally? How can the Trinity be seen as relevant to culture?

H. Richard Niebuhr's *Christ and Culture* delineated five approaches to culture adopted by Christians since New Testament times. Niebuhr brilliantly described five models: Christ against culture, the Christ of culture, the Christ above culture, Christ and culture in paradox and Christ the transformer of culture. The Christ against culture motif was represented, according to Niebuhr, by Tertullian, the Mennonites and Tolstoy who rejected culture, its worth and its claims to the loyalty of Christians. Culture was the province of evil and was irreconcilably alienated from God. The Christ of culture theme, Niebuhr saw preeminently in the Christian Gnostics (i.e. Basilides, Valentinus), Abelard, Ritschl, and Schleiermacher who viewed Jesus as primarily the fulfillment of culture's hopes and aspirations. The Christ above culture mode, was seen in the thought of Clement and Aquinas who sought to synthesize culture with the Christ who is superior to culture. The model of Christ and culture related as in a paradox was exemplified in the dualism of Luther who emphasized the great gulf between sinful human culture and a holy God. Christ as the transformer of culture was apparent in the thought of Augustine, Calvin, and F.D. Maurice most clearly. Though this conversionist perspective also has been present in the thought of other Christian thinkers, Niebuhr believed that Augustine and Calvin most clearly taught and demonstrated the transformation of culture into the Kingdom of God.

Each of Niebuhr's analyses is incisive and scholarly. Yet each historical model he described was successful in challenging its culture only to the degree it went beyond relating Christ to culture and also related the three in one to culture. It must be acknowledged, of course, that most of the Christian thinkers cited by Niebuhr considered themselves to be Trinitarians though they, like many Christians, tended to focus most heavily on Jesus Christ rather than on the three in their theologizing. Augustine, more than most, acknowledged the relation of the three divine persons to culture. The Bishop of Hippo's emphasis on the Triune God was a sharp breach with Classicism.

Augustine traced the Fall of Rome to the defective philosophic orientation of the ancient world. Most Greeks and Romans had sought for the basic principle of reality in the material realm. For many, one or another part of nature was the substantial cause or first principle of reality. Yet they had to explain motion and how it related to their first principle. Consequently, movement (becoming) itself became a second major principle of reality. But then the ancients had to relate motion to their first principle. That connecting link required a third principle of reality. In the quest for first principles, the Greeks spawned numerous philosophies. Heraclitus conceived a materialistic dialectic. Pythagoras developed a mystical idealism. Parmenides and Zeno demonstrated the unintelligibility of motion. A general divergence took place in Greek thought with some finding a first principle in the material world and with others finding it in the inner, subjective world.

It was left to Plato to attempt to unify these perspectives by relating being (ideas or forms) and becoming (motion). He attempted to do so by identifying the ultimately real with ideas which were to be discovered by escaping from sense perception and the material world. He failed, however, to do justice to material reality when he placed the thinking subject in opposition to material objects and to sense perception. And so he and the Neoplatonists, who later influenced Roman thought, led society to believe in a closed natural order whose major deficiency was an inadequate understanding of the relation of transcendence to matter.

According to Augustine, the heart of the problem for the ancients was their belief that the philosophies they had spun were independent and autonomous. They philosophized in a closed cosmic order which they viewed as an end in itself. Whether they saw some element of closed nature as the first principle of reality, whether they included autonomous man as part of that closed natural order, or whether they recognized transcendence in the cosmic order, the bottom line was that for them reality was independent, autonomous, and self sufficient in itself. Their philosophy, their science, their political thought failed to disclose any purpose beyond a closed, natural order. Thus, first principles were bound by the limitations of a closed system and were unable to arbitrate contraries either in the realm of truth or of ethics. Neither were impersonal principles capable of satisfying humanity's insatiable hunger for certitude, for happiness, and for unity.

Augustine's emphasis on the Trinity as the first principle of reality sharply contrasted with the views of the ancient world. For him reality was dependent on the Triune God. The Father, above and beyond all things, was viewed as creative being knowable as He manifests Himself in the Son and Spirit. The Spirit undergirded the principle of motion operating in the realm of becoming. The Son as the logos or principle of intelligence ordered the universe as well as relating being (Father) and becoming (Spirit) without absorbing one into the other. As one, they cannot be separated nor can they become antithetical to each other. They are described as the God who is, who knows, and who wills eternally in total cooperation and in the perfect unity of infinite love. This Trinity, for Augustine, was the only principium who unifies reality, who can unify human perceptions of reality, and who can unify society.

Integral to Augustine's understanding of the Trinity was his awareness of the permeability of the Spirit. The Holy Spirit, and through Him the Father and Son, permeate all of reality. Within the Trinity, there is perichoresis, the interpenetration of each by the others without obscuring the eternal existence and uniqueness of any one. The perichoresis and permeability of the Trinity thus enables the persons of the Triune God to undergird each other and reality. Thus, the Trinity for Augustine was the first principle which replaced the defective arche of Classicism. He called for the Trinity to be a starting point and foundation for a new, Christian social order. The Trinity, with its emphasis on persons would help to humanize society by sacralizing personality. Because of the Trinity's involvement with the natural order, it contained the possibility of bringing about a new appreciation of nature. It was the framework within which science could be renewed as Trinitarian transcendence and freedom dissipated the notion of a closed universe determined by its own laws and opposed to freedom.

A Trinitarian perspective on culture was expressed by Augustine in his *City of God* in which he contrasted two societies one of which is secular, the other of which is Trinitarian. "The one is the city of Christ, the other of the devil; the one of the good, the other of the evil; both composed of angels as well as men." (*Enchiridion*, XXIX) They include all humans and all of history, from the beginning to the end. They mingle together physically but are separated morally and spiritually. They are distinguished from each other by their desires. That which animates secular society is "the love of self to the point of contempt for God; that which animates divine society is the love of God to the point of contempt for self." (*City of God*, XIV, 28) Augustine went on to point out that these conflicting desires may therefore be described respectively as greed and love. The secular city, then, is dominated by a love of possessions. It is where people devour each other like fish in the sea. Conflict, exploitation, and a love of power characterizes the secular world because its citizens love finite, material objects.

On the other hand, the City of God is dominated by the power of love, specifically love from and for the Triune God who is infinite. Since God's love is inexhaustible, there is no conflict or strife among men to secure that which is in infinite supply. Grace is free and unconditioned. It forgives, heals man's inner and outer alienations and prepares him to be part of God's eternal city. So Augustine called people to a vision of the society God wills. That vision was unifying because it was of the one body of Christ. It was true community because it was the communion of saints. It repudiated the prideful, classical ideal of the self-perfectible super man because it admitted that all men are sinners needing divine grace.

The Augustinian model of relating the Trinity to culture is that of two universal cities. The city of God seeks to win the city of the world to its values and to the Triune God who is the source of those values. It seeks to transform the secular by interpenetrating worldly society. The perichoresis in the Godhead is reflected in the permeation of the world by people who participate in the life of the Triune God. The society based on faith seeks to demonstrate how the highest ideals and noblest longings of secular society can be truly fulfilled only by a love relation to the God who is Triune. So Augustine developed a basis for the interaction of Christianity and culture.

Another influential guide in the effort to integrate Christianity and culture was John Calvin. The genius of Geneva was a thorough going Trinitarian whose thought was profoundly informed both by Scripture and by Augustine. His recognition of the independence and self-existence of Father, Son, and Holy Spirit clearly laid to rest any trace of subordinationism in the Trinity. His emphasis on the work of the Spirit in both common and efficacious grace working in the human will and mind has caused some to call him the "Theologian of the Holy Spirit."[1]

Calvin understood that the Holy Spirit both regenerates and sanctifies believers. But He also empowers people who are not believers to have dominion over the earth and to build their cultures (common grace). "For when the Spirit of God is said to dwell only in the faithful, that is to be understood of the Spirit of sanctification by whom we are consecrated as temples to God himself. Yet it is equally by the energy of the same Spirit, that God replenishes, actuates, and quickens all creatures . . . (Insti-

tutes, II,2,16) Calvin held that we ought to appreciate truth wherever it is found since all truth comes from God. A saving knowledge of God comes to the elect only from the Spirit and the Word. But whatever is true in culture or mathematics or science also is a gift of the Spirit who quickens human minds. It is a common grace from God available to all people. It is consistent with but inferior to efficacious grace which saves. Nevertheless, it comes from the Father through the Son by the Holy Spirit. It restrains the evil of mankind while bestowing good gifts upon all who will receive them.

For Calvin, Scripture was the unique, infallible Word of God. Its writers were inspired by the Holy Spirit so that "Scripture is the school of the Holy Spirit" (*Institutes* III,21,3) wherein the elect learn that which is necessary and beneficial. The Holy Spirit inspired Scripture and illuminates believers through it. Thus, we note Calvin's constant references to the Word and the Spirit as related and interactive in guiding and instructing mankind.

The key concept in the Scriptures according to Calvin was the sovereignty of the Triune God. The sovereign Lord redeems the chosen by His saving grace while empowering all people by His common grace. His sovereignty is an attribute which is inextricably bound up with the three persons and all other attributes. By His Word and Spirit, He exercises His sovereignty over all that is. His sovereignty is essential to His transcendence. His sovereignty is His absolute freedom to do whatever He chooses. His immanence is His sovereignty in action. Thus, in His sovereignty being and becoming unite even as in His Incarnation and crucifixion being and becoming also meet.

Belief in the absolute sovereignty of God provided Calvin with the key for integrating culture and Christian values. God's rule is to be extended to all of life. An awareness of God's sovereignty rings the death knell for all forms of absolutism since all powers are seen as subservient to and dependent upon God's power. Kings, potentates, and religious leaders all derive their power from God. Similarly, church and state under God have their own divinely established spheres of responsibility and jurisdiction.

They ought not to violate the conscience of individuals who are accountable to the sovereign Lord alone.

For Calvin, the individual believer, because of grace, enjoys Christian liberty from the bondage of the law. Nothing is unclean in itself. Cultural activities including art, music and literature, economic wealth, the enjoyment of food, drink, and clothing are not in themselves evil. Cultural striving, however, becomes evil if it is directed toward selfish purposes rather than toward the glory of God. But within the framework of God's sovereignty, culture building was seen by Calvin as fulfilling God's cultural mandate. "Be fruitful and multiply, and replenish the earth and subdue it and have dominion . . ." (Genesis 1:28)

Calvin, while highlighting God's sovereignty, joined with Luther in a renewed proclamation of the Biblical message of God's calling. Every man has a calling from God. (*Institutes* III, 10, 6) Every believer is called to be a prophet, priest, and king in Christ. He is to bring all things under the rule of the sovereign Lord. In addition, each person has a role to fill in life. "Every man's life, therefore, is a kind of station assigned him by the Lord." (Ibid) So cultures are built under the sovereignty of the God who calls each person, in his own assigned place, to fulfill the cultural mandate with the assistance of common grace.

Such calling applies not only to believers, but also to nonbelievers. There is a place in God's plan for each person. The Christian who identifies with Christ as prophet, priest, and king must of necessity transform that corner of God's vineyard to which he has been called. But in the common grace of God all people have a calling whether or not they are predestined to salvation. (*Institutes* II, 2, 15–17; II, 3) God as sovereign extends His rule over all things through the calling He issues to all people. As people, consciously or unconsciously, follow His divine purposes, His sovereignty is manifest in the cultures of earth. Culture, in so far as it carries out the mandate of Genesis 1:28, may be viewed as the fulfillment of His sovereignty over creation.

Yet not everything in culture accords with His will. It must be understood that Calvin's affirmation of God's sovereignty does not imply that everything people do in culture building is pleasing to the Almighty. Calvin more than most Christian thinkers recognized man's fall into sin and corruption. Yet human sin cannot annul God's sovereign purposes which will be fulfilled in spite of man's rebellion and disobedience. Though the natural man has become a vagabond upon the earth, he still has the urge to fulfill the cultural mandate. He builds his Babylons though they may oppose God. The very fact that he builds his civilizations, however, establishes his dominion over the creation which though subjected to vanity is waiting to be delivered. (Rom. 8:18) God's sovereignty is not frustrated forever even where it is not acknowledged.

Calvin also developed an ethic which he believed demonstrated not only obedience to the sovereign King of creation, but also reflected His will as revealed by the Holy Spirit in Scripture. He taught the dignity of work. "There will be no employment so mean and sordid as not to appear truly respectable, and be deemed highly important in the sight of God." (*Institutes* III, 10, 6) Every calling, whether that of the scullery maid, the laborer in the fields, or the prince, is of equal honor before God. Work is the essence of man's service to God and to humanity and should be man's highest joy. Work is man's response to God's call to be a fellow worker with Him in the development of the earth. Work then for the Christian is a must. It gives meaning to his life as he serves his Sovereign by replenishing and subduing the earth.

Education also played a significant role in Calvin's view of culture. His founding of the Academy in Geneva demonstrated the importance of learning. But, for him, all true knowledge comes from God. A knowledge of God and of His creation was necessary to obey the cultural mandate. The study of history, the classics, the natural sciences could help to equip believers for serving God. Calvin sought to transplant all legitimate knowledge into a Biblical perspective. All learning was to be used for the glory and service of the sovereign God.

Calvin endeavored to bring all of human culture under the sovereignty of the Triune God by bringing it into conformity to the Holy Spirit-inspired Word of God. The family, the church, the state, the economic order, scholarship, art, leisure are to be brought under the Lordship of Christ. Yet, earthly culture has an eschatalogical aspect also. All of life is preparation for the enjoyment and the service of the culture of heaven where God will be all in all. Though this world and its cultures will pass away, the culture of eternity where God's sovereign will shall be perfectly performed, will abide forever.

In the seventeenth century, the brilliant scientist-philosopher Blaise Pascal also had a vision of reality which can inspire cultural unity. His vision, expanding on the Augustinian perspective, provides another model for an integration of Christianity and culture. Etienne Pascal and his son Blaise had grappled with the question—how do Christianity and culture relate to each other? Blaise, in later years, developed a vision of reality which provided him with a framework within which Christianity and culture could be related. His vision may have developed from seed thoughts planted by his father. They blossomed forth as his understanding of Scripture matured and found confirmation in his own experience. His vision was Trinitarian though it centered in Jesus Christ.

In his great apologetic work, *The Pensees*, Pascal spoke of the incredible complexity of reality and of three all-encompassing orders of reality which, though separated by infinite abysses, are one in God. He described his vision in his doctrine of the three orders:

> "The infinite distance between body and mind is a symbol of the infinitely more infinite distance between mind and charity . . .
> All bodies, the firmament, the stars, the earth and its kingdoms, are not equal to the lowest mind . . .
> All bodies together, and all minds together, and their products, are not equal to the least feeling of charity. This is of an order infinitely more exalted." (Fragment 792)

The lowest order, the material realm, includes not only the starry heavens, the seas and the hills, but also political kingdoms sustained by material power and dynasties built on economic wealth. The rich and powerful rule in this order. (Fr 460) The senses, experimentation, and desire hold sway in the material realm. (Fr 83)

In the material realm, men wander in search of justice, truth and goodness but find only shadows. Nature is incapable of thought. The senses and experimentation lead only to tentative and uncertain conclusions. Nature is blind and provides no ultimate answers. "Nature presents to me nothing which is not a matter of doubt and concern." (Fr 229) This led him to cry out, "The eternal silence of these infinite spaces frightens me." (Fr. 206) The material realm only can be organized and used. By itself, it provides no certain answers to the basic questions of meaning which haunt man.

What then of the second order, the realm of the mind? It is the realm of intellectuals, philosophers and geniuses. According to Pascal, it is separated from unthinking matter by an infinite abyss. It is the glory of man that he thinks. Pascal recognized that some men have the capacity to think mathematically (analytically and extensively), that others think intuitively (synthetically and in depth) while still other "dull" minds think neither mathematically nor intuitively. Pascal pointed out that basic to all man's reasoning are certain first principles such as space, time, motion and number. Reasoning is impossible apart from first principles which are intuitions of the heart. "Principles are intuitive, propositions are inferred." (Fr 282) Pascal thus humbled reason, particularly mathematical reasoning, since it only is possible as it builds on principles derived from intuition.

Pascal further humbled autonomous, human reason by pointing out that it can be led astray by desire, by the senses, by imagination or by illness. He also highlighted reason's finite limitations in the face of infinity. "I hold it . . . impossible to know the parts without knowing the whole." (Fr 72) He went on to point out that autonomous reason leads to contradictions. For example, reason establishes both man's greatness and his baseness, his nobility and his brutishness. "What a chimera is man! What a novelty! What a monster, what a chaos, what a contradiction . . . Judge of all things, imbecile worm of the earth: depositary of truth, a sink of uncertainty and error; the pride and refuse of the universe." (Fr 434) "The greatness of man is great in that he knows himself to be miserable." (Fr 397) Those who dwell in the cul-de-sac of the mind experience bitter contradiction and paradox rather than certainty.

Such contradictions find their resolution, not by autonomous reason, but by answers revealed from the third and highest order of reality which is the realm of holy love (charity). Paradoxes of the mind are untangled by an awareness of the transcendent wisdom which descends from the third order. Separated from the order of the mind by an infinite abyss, the order of love is represented by the saints and supremely by Jesus Christ at the apex of reality. Infinitely removed but presiding over all reality is the Lord of holy love. He has revealed Himself and His wisdom in the history of the Jews, in His incarnation and in Scripture, the doorway to the highest order which is love. "The sole aim of the Scripture is charity." (Fr 669)

The third order of reality is known by the heart. The heart for Pascal was the center of the personality. It includes the feelings and the will. It is the soil out of which comes sound reasoning. Through the heart first principles are known. In the heart, unholy desires can lead men astray. But in the heart God also is felt and then known. A person encounters God in his heart. God inclines the heart to believe. Then one comes to acknowledge God in his mind. When the holy love of the highest order is revealed to a human heart, a person experiences a new wholeness. When a person becomes whole through Divine love, he comes to see the wholeness of reality even as God who is Infinite Wholeness knows reality.

Though Pascal, as he sought to ascend upward through the three orders, experienced them as discontinuous and as separated one from the other by infinite abysses, he saw the three as unified when viewed from the summit of reality. As he climbed painfully through the material and mental orders, he struggled in vain to span the abyss separating them from that which is ultimate. He struggled to understand the resistless change and uncertainty which he discovered in the processes of the material and mental realms. But then grace from the highest order descended to his life. When he came to view reality through eyes of the eternal Christ, he saw culture and all of reality as sublimely unified. Scanning the three orders through the mind of Christ, he saw new unity, new meaning and new constancy in all things. That which had been seen as fragmented and changing now was seen as unified and unchanging in the light of the highest order of Divine love. What made the difference? It was the difference between the perspective from within the lower orders and the perspective from transcendence.

Whereas he once had seen only contradictions and confusion in the realm of the mind, now Pascal saw wisdom and meaning shining from the order of holy love and resolving the contradictions perplexing rational people. In this, he followed Augustine who stated that faith in God was the existential precondition to true rationality and wholeness. For example, Pascal understood the wisdom of God as reconciling those whose reasoning led them to classify man as a brute with those whose reasoning led them to call man angelic. Divine wisdom reminds us that man has fallen into brutishness though before his fall he was angelic. The archetypal remnant of Edenic goodness still lingers in the human psyche struggling against brutish forces unleashed by the Fall. "I created man holy, innocent, perfect . . . He withdrew himself from my rule . . . I abandoned him to himself . . . so that man is now become like the brutes." (Fr 430)

The realm of the mind when illumined by light from the highest order of reality gives meaning and direction for the material order. That light is mediated through Scripture, the Spirit and the church. Divine justice replaces man-made, transitory notions of justice in the world of politics. Divine love and justice inspire a just use of riches in the economic order. The mind and heart purified of selfish impulses reflect accurately the first principles (i.e. order, proportion, et.al.) without which the scientific mind is impotent to analyze the material universe. Where man's disproportion to nature's extremes as well as to the totality of nature once relativised and warped man's knowledge, now man's knowledge is restored as he understands his God-ordained relation to nature. The order of holy love radiates downward into the lesser orders giving them new meaning, purpose, proportion, constancy, and direction. A new point of viewing is given to those who see reality from the summit.

After the mystic night (November 23, 1654) when Pascal's own heart and mind were bathed in the Divine love of the highest order, he saw how man's knowledge, which is distorted by his experience of disproportion to nature and to nature's God, was renewed when man experienced his proper relation to nature as it is revealed from the apex of reality. He came to see the beautiful harmony of the three orders of reality. He understood how the highest order unified, harmonized and interpreted all the orders. He knew that seeing reality through the mind of Christ gave wholeness, unity, constancy and meaning to all the orders of reality. He discovered how the sovereign, third order (divine love) provided the second order (mind) with reliable first principles and conceptual categories which enable it to know and to interpret the first order (the senses and materiality).

Prior to that night of ecstasy, he had known only confusion. He had bumped his head against impassable abysses as he sought to reason his way up the orders of reality. The inconstancy of the senses in the material order led him to illusions. Reason, in the order of the mind, led him only to antinomies and contradictions. Autonomous man, without the grace of the highest order, is a victim of desire, custom and imagination. The finite, thus, wanders in infinite darkness.

Every person is a composite of the lower orders. People today wander in bewilderment as the senses lead them into the morass of relativism and as their minds lead them down deadend pathways to meaningless paradoxes. Autonomous man is lost clutching at strands of insight but unable to weave them into an abiding, sure pattern of meaning. Man's dilemma is that he doesn't know which order of reality ought to be made determinative and authoritative for the others. But those who experience and give first priority to the descending grace of the order of Divine love are able to interpret reality aright. They have a perspective which orders and integrates the facets of culture. Each dimension of reality is given its own integrity, freedom and proper proportion both to man and to God. At the same time each is related to the whole through the Lord who rules over all. Those who existentially experience the grace of the One who rules from the summit of reality are called to relate all of reality and all of culture's ambiguities to the One who unifies all. Pascal's view of the sovereignty of the third order may well provide a perspective within which Christian thinkers may fulfill their cultural mandate to bring every impulse, every thought and every order of reality into captivity to Christ and through Christ and the Spirit to the Father.

Pascal's vision of reality mirrored the Biblical viewpoint. Biblical writers clearly understood the massive rifts which exist between the material world, the domain of the human mind and the transcendent realm of Divine wisdom and grace. Apart from God, autonomous economic and political systems create "crooked and perverse" nations. (Phil. 2:15) Apart from God, nature is without purpose and offers no guidance. Though the imprint of God is upon nature, without God man becomes blind to meaning in nature. "Even as they did not like to retain God in their knowledge, God gave them over to a reprobate mind." (Rom. 1:28) Ever since God "cursed the ground" after the fall (Gen. 3:17), the creation has been "in bondage to decay" and "groaneth and travaileth in pain." (Rom. 8:21-22) Biblical writers, again and again, pointed out that, apart from God, the material realm which is "red in tooth and claw" is alienated both from God and from man.

Apart from God, the intellectual sphere also is alienated and blinded according to Biblical writers. Paul said, "There is none that understandeth." (Rom. 3:11) "You that were sometime alienated and enemies in your mind by wicked works yet now hath he reconciled." (Col. 1:21) "The natural man receiveth not the things of the Spirit of God: for they are foolishness unto him." (I Cor. 2:14) The Psalmist declared, "Such knowledge (of God's love), is too wonderful for me; it is high, I cannot attain unto it." (Ps. 139:6) Isaiah heard God saying, "My thoughts are not your thoughts, neither are your ways my ways, saith the Lord. For as the heavens are higher than the earth, so are my ways higher than your ways, and my thoughts than your thoughts." (Isa. 55:8,9) Biblical teaching describes the infinite gulf between man's finite reasonings which are warped and blinded by his faulted ego and God's infinite knowledge and glorious wisdom.

The Bible, though recognizing the inability both of the natural order and of the intellectual order to bridge the gaps and to ascend to God, joyfully announces that the Triune God has condescended both to undergird and to reveal Himself in nature and in human history. Viewed from the vantage point of finitude, infinite abysses block the ascent to God. Viewed from the summit of reality, God's sovereign presence and power permeate and unify all things. Humanity is called to identify with God through Christ. From that cleansing perspective, all things are seen as one in God.

The contemporaneity of Pascal's vision may be demonstrated by its similarity to Teilhard de Chardin's description of the cosmic process in the 20th century. According to Teilhard, under Divine impulses a noosphere (a global intertwining of human minds) has evolved from the biosphere which in turn has evolved from physical nature. Like Pascal, his fellow Auvergnat, Chardin recognized the existence of the physical order (including the biological), the noosphere (the realm of mind) and the order of Divine love. Like Pascal, he gave priority to the Christly order of Divine love which surges through the whole cosmic process. Viewing all reality from the perspective of the Omega point of Christ who rules from the future of all history, Chardin was enthralled with the unity given to all things by Christ.

Pascal discovered that when reality is viewed from the perspective of sovereign, transcendent holy love, the order of the mind is given a framework, an unchanging goal, sure conceptual categories, and a firm presuppositional basis for its cogitations. The order of the mind then can analyze, understand and organize the material realm in the light of transcendent goals and purposes. The mind, cleansed and healed by contact with holy love, then perceives that reality has rationality and intelligibility inherent in it because God pervades all reality. The human mind which views reality from the perspective of divine holy love comes to understand that the divine rationality pervading all things was prior to human rationality. Therefore, the world and rational endeavor have been given an integrity and a divinely rooted autonomy of their own. Pascal reminds us that the perspective of Christ, as it is made known in Scripture, is the only reasonable alternative to being swallowed up by the darkness and silence of the swirling abysses which fragment reality. Pascal reminds us, as did Calvin, that all things are to be brought into harmony through subjection to the sovereign Lord. Pascal reminds us, as did Augustine, that the Trinity ruling from the peak of reality provides the resolution of the contradictions and dilemmas of the intellectual, political, economic and scientific realms.

In the twentieth century, Tubingen's Karl Heim also was concerned about the rift between Christianity and culture. He related insights from the Bible and from theology to contemporary scientific and philosophic notions. In the process he developed a framework for relating Christianity and culture which has some parallel to that depicted by Pascal. The major difference, however, is that Pascal's emphasis was Christological and Trinitarian whereas Heim's, though theistic, was not explicitly Trinitarian.

Heim saw reality comprised of various "spaces." There is the objective space of physical matter. Then there is the non-objective space of person to person relations where "I" interacts with "Thou" through the objective world. These two spaces make up polar space[2] which exists in three dimensions (length, width, height). All physical objects, all creatures, and all humans exist in these three dimensions. Heim inferred from the work of Bolyai, Lobachevski, and Reimann that there is an infinite number of spaces and dimensions above and beyond the three dimensions of polar space. Yet he posited the existence of a limitless, ultimate dimension which he called suprapolar space. The ultimate space is the omnipresence of God, the one facet of the infinite God which is comprehensible to creation. Heim avoided the error of describing God as part of the universe by defining suprapolar space as the point of contact between the Infinite God and creation. Suprapolar space transcends, but encloses all other spaces. It is related to but distinct from other spaces. Heim put it, "each space possesses a structure which is fundamentally different from the structures of all other spaces. Consequently, any two spaces are separated from one another by an immense gulf."[3]

Heim's notion of separated spaces, which he borrowed from science, parallels Pascal's concept of orders each of which is separated by an abyss from the others. Heim's understanding of suprapolar space parallels Pascal's understanding of the order of love. Heim points out, like Pascal, how everything is transformed when one views reality after the discovery of suprapolar space.[4] A major difference between Pascal and Heim occurs in Heim's description of the center of vision. Whereas Pascal views all reality from the order of love and sees all things through the eyes and mind of Christ, Heim asserts that the center of vision "is my own ego"[5] albeit a new ego. Pascal centers all things around a Christological and Trinitarian perspective whereas Heim's suprapolar space, although including the personal, is not the center of reality.

We may learn much from Heim. Could it be that his understanding of the omnipresence of God as suprapolar space provides a clue to a new understanding of the Trinity? Could it be that Pascal's order of love, Heim's suprapolar space, and the contemporary scientist's understanding of dimension suggest a concept which makes the three eternal persons in God more comprehensible to modern culture? Could it be that one aspect of the Triune God is the ultimate dimension of reality, transcending yet undergirding creation, enfolding yet different from reality? Could it be that within God are three equal, suprapersonal "dimensions" which interpenetrate each other (perichoresis) and yet which are eternally distinct and different? Just as the impersonal dimensions we experience, length and breadth and height, permeate each other yet are distinct from each other, so infinite suprapersons and the suprapersonal "dimensions" they create may permeate each other, being mutually dependent and mutually exclusive, without losing identity. Just as suprapolar space may encompass and permeate all lower spaces without absorbing or being absorbed by them, similarly the transcendent Trinity enfolds all reality in its suprapersonal love and power without absorbing or being absorbed by it.

Such a view translates into a deepened understanding of God's relations to His universe. It enables the secularist's view of reality to coexist with the Christian's view. It legitimatizes both though it maintains that the Christian sees reality more comprehensively and more exhaustively. The secularist views the death of a friend merely in polar, three dimensional (length, height, width), positivistic terms. The Christian views the same death in polar terms but also in the light of the suprapolar perspective of the eternal Triune God. Similarly the secularist views Jesus' resurrection or any other miracle described in the Bible from a strictly three dimensional perspective. The Christian views such miracles both from a three dimensional and from a higher-dimensional perspective. He sees Jesus' dead body in three dimensional terms. But he also sees the reaction of startled, believing disciples in terms of non-objectifiable space of personal relationships. In addition, the Christian views the resurrection in light of God's eternal presence and power (suprapolar space). Reality, like an onion composed of one layer after another layer, is composed of one dimension after another dimension. Everything that is or happens in reality exists in a multidimensional mode and can be viewed from the perspectives of various dimensions. So a sunrise may be described from within a time-space perspective or from within the multidimensional perspective of the Trinity. The former would analyze the sunset's astronomical, geographical, meteorological, and chemical/physical factors. The latter would deal with its creation, beauty, meaning, and influence on people. The sunset participates in the dimensions of physical existence (objective, three-dimensional space), of non-objective finite, personal being (the self of the observers) and of divine reality (the Father as the source of reality; the Spirit as the undergirding presence in all reality). These dimensions all converge in and permeate the sunset though each retains its own independent existence.

The complementarity of dimensions in a multidimensional universe may possibly explain how some legitimately may describe reality in a strictly empirical manner while others legitimately may depict reality in a Trinitarian fashion. The Trinitarian explanation includes the descriptions made available by all the lower dimensions while going beyond them to become the most comprehensive and complete explanation known to man. In the Trinitarian vision of reality, all lesser perspectives are harmonized and unified. The perspectives of lower dimensions, by themselves, lead either to contradictions or to meaningless abysses. From the Trinity comes a splendid unity and a magnificent completeness which infuses all reality.

In the modern world, how does this vision of the Trinity relate to society? What values, generated by the Triune God, can direct contemporary life? It has been made clear that God is differentiated. He is Father, Son, and Holy Spirit. Each person is eternally distinct from the others.

Differentiation permeates all reality as God the Father begets all things through His Son and as the Holy Spirit undergirds, sustains, and drives the cosmos toward the Son and the Father. (Cf. Chardin) A differentiated God has created, sustains, and moves a differentiated universe.

Seen from the human point of view, as Pascal pointed out, differentiations in reality (i.e. matter, mind, spirit) are separated by vast, impassable abysses. Seen from the summit of reality where sovereign love rules, all things are interrelated, mutually interdependent and one in God. Just as the differentiations in God (three persons) are one in their infinite love, so reality with its multitudinous parts has a wholeness and oneness in God. That oneness amidst differentiation is expressed in the Trinity and in the perichoresis and interpenetration of the persons one with the other. The dimensionality of the divine persons enables them to permeate each other in love. Similarly, the differentiations and dimensions in reality are able to interrelate in the unity and community God gives to reality.

Reality, like the Triune God, is differentiated yet marvelously interrelated and unified in Him. Reality reflects the community in God. Reality, seen in light of the Triune God, fits together like a completed jig saw puzzle. The differentiations are wonderously complementary to each other. Each expresses, fulfills, and completes the others. Each needs the others. Even more gloriously than the complementarity of the Chinese yin and yang or of the Zoroastrian light and darkness, the persons of the Trinity complement and fulfill each other. In turn, the differentiations in reality, when viewed from the divine perspective, complement each other.

Analogically, society when studied in light of the Trinitarian reality, is differentiated. The abysses which seem to separate and to fragment a differentiated humankind and the values it generates can be overcome only by experiencing the sublime love, sovereignty, unity, community, complementarity, and perichoresis of the Triune God. In God and the values He reflects into society through His Body and its members, there is hope that true community may be realized to some degree upon the earth.

The Trinity, then, may be the ultimate paradigm which could guide Christians in transforming the cultures of earth. According to Thomas S. Kuhn, "a paradigm is what the members of a scientific community share."[6] Transposing his definition into a theological context, a paradigm would be what Christians share. Christians may hold different doctrines. They may live different life styles. They may advocate different political or economic philosophies. But all believers participate in the community of the Trinity. They share in the sovereign love of the Father, Son, and Spirit.

Kuhn also has pointed out that "a paradigm governs, in the first instance, not a subject matter but rather a group of practitioners."[7] If the Trinity is the paradigm which can direct the Christian community in changing culture, it must govern, dominate and sovereignly rule the lives of believers. Though Christians still may differ in their understandings of how the divine paradigm specifically applies to culture, such differences can be creative. Out of the diverse theoretical applications conceived by Christians will emerge those which prove that they actually are relevant and do, in fact, apply to diverse situations and diverse cultures. Eventually, diverse applications which stand the test of time will come to be seen as complementary to each other, increasing the richness of the new community.

What we are suggesting, then, is that the Triune God, described by Biblical writers, interpreted by Augustine and the church, and applied to life by Calvin, Pascal, and others may be the ultimate theological paradigm which can recreate the cultures of earth. The Trinity, sovereign love ruling all reality, the supreme unity amidst diversity, the sublime community of love, is the hope for the renewal of culture.

NOTES

[1] Warfield, B.B. *Calvin and Calvinism*, (New York: Oxford University Press, 1931), p. 21.

[2] In the development of geometry, the notion of space is undefined and presupposed. The properties of a space are developed, however, through axioms.

[3] Heim, Karl. *Christian Faith and Natural Science*, (New York: Harper and Bros., 1953), p. 169.

[4] Ibid., p. 175.

[5] Ibid., p. 176.

[6] Kuhn, Thomas S. *The Structure of Scientific Revolutions*, (Chicago: University of Chicago Press, 1970), p. 176.

[7] Ibid., p. 180.

6

The Trinity and the World

The Triune God is the source of all that is. He is equally near and equally distant from all things. All things center in Him. He undergirds and permeates all things and all peoples. All the peoples of the world interact with Him even when they do not recognize Him. His is the invisible power giving life and existence to all creation. The Father is the creator and source of the power that surges through all creation. The Son is the Father's wisdom—ordering, structuring, and directing reality. The Spirit is the creative power who is the soul and the center of all things.

The Biblical drama describes the Triune God as He interacts with His creation. Genesis 1 describes how God freely and lovingly willed to create (the Hebrew word is bara) by bringing forth what was not there before (creation ex nihilo). Genesis 1:1 says God created the whole cosmos. Beginning with verse 2 the writer uses the Hebrew verb "to make" (asah) which describes His shaping, forming, patterning what He had created to suit his purposes. The Triune God shaped creation by His Word. "And God said 'Let there be...'" The Word (Christ) links the Creator God with His creation. The Word, the Logos, communicates coherence, meaning, structure and purpose to the whirling world of finite matter and finite intelligences. The Word is the bridge between God the Father and what He created. The Son, who is the perfect Word, eternally expressing the Father, "made" (asah) light and darkness, day and night, heaven and earth by giving each its existence, its form, its structure and order. He made creation so that it expressed God's nature, glory, and purpose.

The Bible also describes God as giving humans a mandate for

building culture.[1] "Be fruitful and multiply and fill the earth and subdue it and have dominion over the fish of the sea and over the birds of the air and over every living thing that moves upon the earth." (Gen. 1:28) God intends humans, since they bear some remnant of the image of the Triune God, to bring all of life into harmony with its Creator. Man, as he builds culture, is to be guided by that which transcends him. He is to unearth the treasures of nature and to shape them for the enrichment of human life and for the glory of God. Humans then, are intended to continue the work of the Creator, to work with, to shape, and to subdue the wonders of creation which reflect something of God's nature and purpose.

The apostle declared, "Ever since the creation of the world, his invisible nature, namely, his eternal power and deity has been clearly perceived in the things that have been made" (Romans 1:20). Those with open minds, as they interact with nature, can discover intimations (not proofs) of God's nature, power and lordship. As they observe nature, they note persistent orderliness pervading the infinitely small and the infinitely large. They see order, which is presupposed by all science, in the interrelatedness and unity of creation. Such order suggests that there is an all powerful Creator who is the source of order.

Since order implies intelligence, people also can see suggestions of a superintelligence overshadowing and underlying the natural order. As they seek assurance that the perception of reality registered in their minds actually corresponds to the world around them, many have sensed that a superior intelligence links the human mind to the external world. Without the divine mind bridging between human minds and an orderly universe, humans have no adequate basis for confidence that their mental images of the world correspond to the world they live in.

As people interact with nature, many also have seen intimations that contingency and dependency pervade all things. They can experience two facets of contingency. They experience a sense of awe which suggests that the ordered cosmos is not self-sufficient, self-contained, and closed but that it is open to something unchangeable beyond itself upon which it depends for its existence. Yet they also have an awareness that this contingent universe which seems to point beyond itself has its own existence.

The reality of matter and a sense of the rationality and contingency which underlies order in the universe have caused many to assume that the cosmos came into being by an intelligent Creator. In Judaism these assumptions became convictions that the universe had a distinct beginning and that its orderliness was due to the faithfulness and constancy of its Creator and Sustainer. Later, Christian thinkers viewed the physical world as real and as having its own independent but open existence because they saw God incarnate intruding into it and subjecting Himself to it. Consequently, culture influenced by Christianity came to regard the empirical world seriously and reverently.

Outside of the Christian tradition, people also have struggled to come to grips with the orderliness, intelligibility/rationality, and contingency of nature. In all parts of the world, people have sought to interpret the natural world which surrounds them. Alan Watts, even though he oversimplifies, may be close to the truth when he says that "the West views the world as artifact (something made), India views the world as drama (something manifested), while China views the world as an organism (something grown)."[2] People in all parts of the world have sensed order, intelligibility and contingency in the natural order and have interpreted the universe in various ways.

The Hindus who are incredibly diverse in their understandings give some evidence of a belief in a creation. The Rg Veda's creation hymn speaks of a time before creation when there was no being and no nonbeing. "Nonbeing then existed not nor being."[3] The hymn concludes on the note that creation's origin is uncertain. Mahayana Buddhism, though world denying, affirms the importance of dharma (cosmic order) where everything determinate depends on something else. Some Mahayana Buddhists have taught that beyond the world is only emptiness. But other teachings suggest that there may exist an agent of creation. The teaching is widespread in the Orient that the world is a manifestation either of Brahman or of the nature of Buddha. The *Vendanta Sutra*, for example, states that Brahman is that from which the world comes, that there is a creative, indeterminate ground of being from which the universe is derived. The *Tao Te Ching* of China contains similar teaching. Lao Tzu pointed out that both being and nonbeing come from a nameless ground. "The Nameless is the origin of Heaven and Earth."[4]

In his *The Idea of the Holy*, Rudolf Otto described the "creature consciousness" or "creature feeling" which people everywhere experience as they are confronted by a mysterious something or someone outside themselves upon whom, they feel, all things depend. He believed that at the core of every religion is an "unnamed Something," a numinous reality which evokes strong feelings in people. "It is the emotion of a creature, submerged and overwhelmed by its own nothingness in contrast to that which is supreme above all creatures."[5] Otto suggested that an emotion of creatureliness comes upon humans when they are confronted by the mysterium tremendum, the majestic awefulness, the immense energy and urgency of the numinous wholly other. He endorsed Schleiermacher's claim that "wherever a mind is exposed in a spirit of absorbed submission to impressions of 'the universe,' it becomes capable . . . of experiencing 'intuitions' and 'feelings' of something that is, as it were, a sheer overplus, in addition to empirical reality."[6] Otto termed these cognitions as "modes of knowing". . . "the intuitive outcome of feeling." He suggested that in people, who are open to the vast realm of nature, feelings of dependence, fear and dread may arise which point them to some mysterious, holy reality upon which all things depend.

Otto pointed out that such cognitions were not innate but were a priori cognitions which all people were capable of having. Everyone shares to varying degrees in a "universal predisposition" which is a "receptivity and a principle of judgment and acknowledgement"[7] which does not produce the a priori cognitions but which is the soil out of which they can arise.

Earlier Immanuel Kant had described the human mind as containing categories and intuitions which shaped knowledge.

But knowledge was dependent upon empirical data. Otto went beyond Kant to suggest that the mind is an instrument which also forms religious ideas and feelings. He spoke of an inward disposition and a religious impulsion to which external stimuli and "pressure from within the mind" both contribute.[8]

As the experiences of life impinge upon humans around the globe, they affect and shape people's existence. Life and death, pain and sorrow, suffering and joy, ugliness and beauty, darkness and light sometimes overwhelm people producing a variety of emotions in the human psyche. Sometimes they evoke terror, dread, awe, joy or guilt. In the instant that one feels crushed and overwhelmed by the power of the aweful, his defenses are down and he becomes vulnerable, weak, open to the unspeakably mysterious. Otto speaks of that aweful awareness of an overpowering reality as an experience of the numinous, an awareness of the mysterium tremendum.

When a human is humbled or broken by guilt or death or tragedy or joy or overwhelming beauty or awesome majesty and power, if he is open and surrendered, he may come face to face with a totally new experience of that to which he has never before been conditioned. In that instant, whether he realizes it or not, he is confronted by a wholly other reality arising from within, descending from above or entering from around him. In such a moment, he becomes aware of a sovereignty beyond him and of his own creaturehood.

In that moment, he may respond to the approach of the Infinite by clenching his fists and closing his spirit in self-centered panic, fear, and defensiveness. Or he may wilt and collapse in self-centered despair. Either alternative leaves him lost before the inexpressible. Or he may let go of self and bow in fear and trembling to surrender self to the awesome and fearsome mysterious confronting him.

If he chooses the route of humble surrender and obedience to whatever righteousness he knows, a presence and a power may arise within his psyche to deepen his awareness of the numinous, to nurture it into a feeling that behind it are personal qualities empathetic to his own personhood. If he continues to respond with surrender and obedience, he may be drawn into a recognition that beyond the universe is justice and mercy. He may be led to repentance and faith in a personal presence beyond the numinous.

Some suggest that such may be the route sincere, selfless persons have followed to experience the invisible Christ even when they have not known His name or His historical acts. Karl Rahner called them "anonymous Christians." Jesus *is* the only way to God since He alone has borne the sins of the world, but some believe that there are people who have encountered Jesus without knowing His name or His acts. The tragedy is, if such be the case, they do not have the full release and joy which a knowledge of Jesus' sacrifice on the cross can bring. Yet their experience may have brought them very close to Him. From a Christian perspective, such experiences suggest that all who experience the numinous are being touched by the Holy Spirit who seeks to open their eyes to His presence in the natural order.

When we consider the teachings of the Hindus, of Buddha, Confucious, Lao-Tzu, and Muhammed, we find insights which may have been derived from such encounters. Among the Hindus are numerous philosophies, various theologies and a host of symbolic stories which describe experiences of the numinous. For example there is a story about the god Vishnu and the man Narada. They were feeling the heat of the desert. Lord Vishnu handed a brass jug to Narada and sent him to an oasis about half an hour's distance to fetch water. At the oasis Narada met a beautiful dark haired woman and her family who cared for him so well that he forgot his lord. Time passed, he married the girl and eventually inherited the parents' treasures. After twelve years, floods swept away his possessions and his family and he was caught in the rushing waters. Suddenly he opened his eyes and found himself in the arms of Vishnu who tenderly asked about the water Narada had promised to bring Lord Vishnu.

Such a story symbolizes the great thirst in the desert of life, the human abandonment of higher obligations in favor of the material comforts and pleasures of life, the flood which sweeps away all earthly support and the compassion of the One who receives his erring servants. Thirst, need, loss are experienced by people who live in a world of fear and dread. Yet in the midst of such terrible feelings some have had an awareness that someone lovingly and patiently waits to receive the erring person.

The author of the story, wandering in the desert of life, must have felt thirst, the fascination of selfish creature comforts, the terror of seeing everything he loved swept away, the sense of being overwhelmed in the threatening flood. Yet in the storm of emotion, he also had encountered a numinous presence which he sensed loved him and forgave him. He attributed to the numinous the name of the Vishnu.

Though certain forms of Hinduism may reflect experiences of a compassionate deity, other forms deal only with abstract philosophic notions. Still other forms speak of innumerable deities (estimated to be 330 million) and their avataras or incarnations. Some of them are terrible and ugly. (i.e. Ganesh, the elephant headed one) Three high gods are Vishnu, Krishna, and Siva. In the Bhagavad Gita, Krishna is depicted as reflecting some characteristics of the mysterium tremendum, the wholly other who evokes feelings of powerlessness and creaturehood.

"Arujna
Made obeisance and spoke yet again to Krishna,
Stammering, greatly affrighted, bowing down."

"O infinite Lord of Gods, in whom the world dwells
Thou the imperishable, existent, non-existent, and beyond both."

"Bowing and prostrating my body,
I beg grace of Thee, the Lord to be revered:
As a father to his son, as a friend to his friend
As a lover to his beloved, be pleased to show mercy. O God."

Krishna responds,
"Because thou art greatly loved of Me
Therefore I shall tell thee what is good for thee.

Be Me-minded, devoted to Me;
Worshipping Me, revere Me;

And to Me alone shalt thou go; truly to thee
I promise it—thou art dear to Me"⁹

Those in this tradition who encountered the numinous or wholly other were aware of someone's grace and mercy. Though they may have clothed their feelings with the symbolism of Krishna, they may have experienced a facet of the divine reality.

Krishna, however, was seen as an incarnation of Vishnu who pervades the whole world with goodness. Vishnu holds symbols in his four hands. The lotus blossom and the battle club bespeak the beautiful, powerful orderliness of the universe which flows from Vishnu. The discus expresses the victorious power of Vishnu. The conch shell represents water and the womb both of which give life.

Siva, in contradistinction to Krishna and Vishnu, is transcendent and full of wrath—a destroyer. Siva destroys in order to recreate. He is part male—part female. He is awesome power and mystery whose worshippers see themselves as most pitiable.

As an ancient hymn sung by Siva's followers puts it:

"Evil, all evil, my race, evil my qualities all.
Great am I only in defects, evil is even my good.
Evil my innermost self, foolish, avoiding the pure.
Beast I am not yet the ways of the beast I never forsake."¹⁰

The followers of Siva, the wholly other, grovel before him, overwhelmed by their creatureliness in the face of such power and cruelty. A severe asceticism has grown out of their experience of dread and awefulness before the numinous.

Emerging out of Hinduism came Buddhism. About 560 B.C., Siddhartha Gautama was born in northeastern India. In his youth, he was protected by his father from any glimpse of people who suffered. He came, however, to the realization that everyone will age, sicken, and die when he was confronted by an old person, a sick person, a beggar, and a corpse. Overwhelmed by dread, Gautama turned to asceticism but found no release. Through a series of dreams, however, he reached the conclusion that through meditation he could break through the cycle of suffering and death. Under a sacred tree, he achieved detachment from his senses and feelings; achieved a new alertness of mind; transcended pain, pleasure, and desire. This was his great awakening. He remained under the tree for seven weeks of bliss and came forth the Buddha, a being awakened to the reality underlying decay and death.

Dread of suffering and death had brought about an encounter between his spirit and the numinous. Gautama is reported as saying: "There is O monks an Unborn, neither become nor created nor formed."[11] For Buddha there was an unknowable which both evoked dread and pain and which offered enlightenment, release, and eternal happiness to people wandering amidst suffering.

Buddhism has taken many twists and turns throughout its long and revered history. The Theravadan Buddhism of Southeast Asia probably represents the oldest Buddhist tradition.

Theravada, depicting Gautama only as a great man and exemplar, teaches that humans, by human effort, must disentangle themselves from life and after several rebirths may achieve release from all suffering. The Mayahana Buddhism of Japan, Korea, and China, while viewing Gautama as both a man and also a manifestation of the ultimate, sees the love of the Buddha as available to save humanity and all creation from the endless round of rebirths from suffering to suffering. The Mayahana ideal is to help to redeem others from this world of suffering. Theravadans, however, see their goal to be achieving Nirvana and leaving this life.

Though Buddhism may have emerged from Gautama's painful encounter with the numinous, many of his followers have become entangled with the selfish aspects of their cultures. At the same time, others by the openness and selflessness of their response to the numinous have been brought to new encounters with the numinous which have brought them an awareness that one facet of the unknowable is grace and mercy.

In China, the thought of Confucious dominated the people for almost twenty five hundred years. Was there any encounter with the numinous which gave rise to his ethical teachings? Though Confucious (K'ung Ch'iu) left little in writing that would indicate a personal encounter with the numinous, he had experiences which made him deeply aware of his creatureliness. His divorce, his loneliness, the death of his mother, his mourning her for three years, his pilgrimage through a China filled with strife, his exile at age fifty-six, the deaths both of his two dearest disciples and of his son all were experiences which humbled him and may well have brought him close to an experience of numinous reality.

It certainly was true that he was conscious of values higher than human values. He was convinced he was "following the Decree of Heaven and was supported by Heaven."[12] What did he mean by Heaven since ancient Chinese thinkers meant numerous things when they used the word? Hear him: "He who sins against Heaven has no place left to pray;" "Alas Heaven has bereft me!" (Words of Confucious upon the death of his favorite disciple); "I make no complaint against Heaven, nor blame men, for though my studies are lowly my mind soars aloft. And that which knows me, is it not Heaven?"[13] Commenting on these texts, the distinguished Chinese scholar Fung Yu Lan has said: "For Confucious, Heaven was a purposeful Supreme Being." Confucious, according to Professor Fung, "believed that he had a holy mission which had been conferred on him by Heaven."[14] Others had a similar view of Confucious. A local official in a small frontier town put it: "The world for long has been without principles. But now Heaven is going to use the Master as an arousing tocsin."[15]

Confucious seemed to have a sense of destiny, a sense of reverence and a sense of awe born of a creaturely encounter with the numinous realm of Heaven. This seems to be evident in his words: "The Superior Man holds three things in awe. He holds the Will of Heaven in awe; he holds the great man in awe; and he holds the precepts of the Sages in awe."[16] Growing out of his experiences, a humbled Confucious gave strong priority in his teaching to the virtues of human heartedness, uprightness, and genuineness (truth).

Closely linked to Confucian thought was Mo-Tzu (Mo Ti) who reacted against some of Confucious' followers. (i.e. Mencius, who viewed Heaven as merely ethical in nature.) He declared that morality depends upon a right relation to the supernatural. Though he held that love is the only way to save the world, he did not believe human nature is capable of love apart from the love of Heaven. Mo Tzu put it: "Thereupon the Will of Heaven proclaimed: All those whom I love they love also . . . But how do we know Heaven loves the people? Because it gives all of them enlightenment."[17] The humble, ascetic Mo Tzu may have been deeply into an understanding of the numinous as love.

Another important strand of Chinese thought arose from the book entitled the *Lao Tzu* or popularly known as the *Tao Te Ching*. It was written sometime after Confucious and became the source of Taoism. Tao (the road or the way) is the all-embracing principle which produces all things. The *Lao Tzu* describes it: "There is a thing, formless yet complete. Before Heaven and Earth it existed. . . . One may think of it as the mother of all beneath Heaven. We do not know its name, but we term it Tao."[18] Further, "Man's standard is Earth. Earth's standard is Heaven. Heaven's standard is Tao. Tao's standard is the spontaneous."[19] Thus, Tao's presence and action are in all things. As the *Lao Tzu* says, "Tao never does, yet through it all things are done."[20] But Tao is not an object. It is both Being and Non-being. They are two aspects of Tao. Non-being is its essence. Being is its function. The *I Ching* says, "One yin and one yang constitute the Tao."[21] Professor Fung, in commenting on the Tao said, "the trinity is the yin, the yang and the harmony resulting from the interaction of these two." He cited the *Chuangtzu*, "The perfect yin is majestically passive. The perfect yang is powerfully active. . . . The interaction of the two forms a harmony from which things are produced."[22] Tao unites possibility and potentiality, yin and yang, Being and Non-being.

Taoism contributed greatly to the Chinese appreciation of harmony in nature. It stressed the notion that men ought to find the natural way to do things. Tao is the good law of nature which men ought to follow to discover the harmony between nature and mankind. It exposes humanity to the numinous.

Early teachers of Taoism, as they faced the world of nature, experienced something of a creaturely feeling as they encountered the mysterium tremendum, the nameless, the Tao. The mysterium tremendum probably is more of a central theme in Taoism than in most other religions. The result is a profound sense of primitive creatureliness. *Lao-Tzu* said, "Mine is the heart of a very idiot. So dull am I. . . . I seem unsettled like the ocean, blown adrift, never brought to a stop."[23]

While those Chinese teachers were discovering their ignorance and finitude, they also became aware of the nameless, the numinous which they called the Tao which is empty of desire, action and thought yet which permeates and produces order in all things. Some have suggested that there is a similarity between the Tao and the logos of both Greek and Christian literature. Were Chinese who were open and surrendered to the majesty of nature encountering something of Him whom Christians worship? After all, as cited earlier, Paul said, "his eternal power and deity have been clearly perceived in the things that have been made. (Romans 1:20)

We also find a sense of the numinous and of human creatureliness in Islam. Muhammed experienced it in his famous vision outside of Mecca. For years he had traveled the lonely desert spaces brooding and pondering existence. Then while praying and fasting on a desert hill near Mecca, he heard a voice saying "O Muhammed Thou art Allah's messenger and I am Gabriel." Whichever way he turned, he saw a bright vision of the angel. Muhammed was overwhelmed and distressed. He soon came to the realization of man's finiteness before the awesome sovereignty of Allah. Muhammed's travels across vast deserts had given him an awareness both of the unity and greatness of God as well as the tininess of man. Like Abraham, Moses and Elijah whom he revered, Muhammed felt deeply the vast gulf between God and man. Through a long succession of revelations, the unity and sovereignty of God came to be expressed in the symbols, metaphors, concepts and paradigms of the Koran.

Hundreds of millions have followed Muhammed in submission to what he believed about God. He developed teachings which said all things are ordered by Allah and that all things are fatalistically predestined by Him. He accentuated man's creaturely dependence on God but offered no dynamic which could enable humans to make progress. His knowledge of Christianity was limited and distorted so he rejected the Triunity of God, considering it blasphemous. But in so doing, he failed to discover the dynamism which could enable him and his followers to fulfill all the implications of submission to God.

Muhammed and millions of Muslims have felt the touch of the numinous and have sincerely expressed both their sense of creatureliness and of the divine sovereignty in teachings which have shaped Islamic culture. They like other peoples of the world may have touched the hem of God's garment.

As humans all over the world have experienced the numinous underlying and transcending nature, they have responded according to the light they have had. It *is* certain that all human beings have awesome experiences of ineffable mystery when they become overwhelmed by certain crisis situations in life. Yet humankind seems to be endowed with an insatiable drive to find meaning in such experiences. The human psyche seems to have a capacity to transform emotional experiences in life into symbols and metaphors which express a person's conscious or unconscious encounter with the Infinite. Could this capacity for symbolization, which is a foundational form of thought, be what Otto meant when he spoke of "pressures from within the mind" which contribute to peoples' religious impulses, understandings and expressions. Susan Langer put it, "the brain is following its own law; it is actively translating experiences into symbols in fulfillment of a basic need to do so." She said, "Ideas are undoubtedly made out of impressions—out of sense messages from the special organs of perception and vague, visceral reports of feeling . . . The material furnished by the senses is constantly wrought into symbols, which are our elementary ideas."[24]

Could it be that people in India and China and throughout the world, having experienced the numinous presence of God's universal Spirit have sought the meaning of that aweful experience? That the symbol-making capacity within them has transformed their experiences into religious impulses, rituals and thoughts which gave rise to the various religions of mankind? Could it be that some of the leaders of those religions may have encountered something of the invisible Christ and that they expressed their experience of Him in symbols which speak of the universal God's creative power and loving mercy?

It seems as though the minds of people everywhere are endowed with a capacity to transform their numinous experiences into symbols, myths, and metaphors intended both to represent the reality they experience and to interpret its meaning. Dr. Sallie McFague has aptly described metaphors as essential for thought and discussion. She has cited Jacob Bronowski, a philosopher of science, who declared, "the whole of science is shot through and through with metaphors. . . . All our ideas derive from and embody such metaphorical likenesses."[25] She also quotes biblical scholar George Caird who said, "all, or almost all, of the language used by the Bible to refer to God is metaphor."[26] The symbols, myths and metaphors which the mind produces are born out of human experiences intermingled with the symbols, myths and metaphors of their culture. What distinguishes the great religious teachers of humankind is their capacity to articulate symbols, myths and metaphors which transcend and go radically beyond the old symbols, myths and metaphors of their cultures.

What makes articulation of their experiences with the numinous effective and appealing is the internal consistency of their symbols and metaphors as well as their comprehensiveness. Their various symbols, myths and metaphors, to a greater or lesser degree, fit together into a consistent, integrated whole. They complement each other to express a rich though partial awareness of reality as they have experienced it. At the same time, they are comprehensive in that they deal with the various strands of the human experience including those which appear to be contradictory. They have found a way to make seeming contradictions bearable.

In addition, what gives such symbols, myths and metaphors seeming validity is that they seem to give people meaning and understanding to light their lives. People tend to respond to such teachers with "that makes sense."

Consequently, the process moves on to transform symbols, myths and metaphors into concepts and ideas which can inform and direct culture. There is risk involved, however, in developing myths and metaphors into concepts. The risk is that concepts often become rigid and inflexible losing some of the dynamism and personal qualities which were first experienced by the great teachers.

The concepts developed by the followers of the great teachers often have become entrapped by the concepts of their culture thus losing some of their radical newness. In the Judeo-Christian tradition this was seen in the loss of dynamism when the rabbis sought to intellectualize Moses, when scholastic Thomists sought to categorize Thomas and when scholastic Lutherans and Calvinists tried to codify and systematize Luther and Calvin.

Whenever symbols, myths and metaphors have been expressed in dynamic concepts which transparently reflected the numinal experiences of great teachers; whenever those concepts have not been captured by old cultural symbols, they have reflected some vitality and meaning to people. Paul Ricoeur has pointed out that thought (concepts) must keep in constant touch with the experiences and symbols which originally inspired and informed them.

Concepts have become bonded together to form some paradigm, a religious framework, a set of basic assumptions which has helped to reshape culture. Such paradigms have provided a total context within which people could live and work and play. Such paradigms reflexively have affected, sharpened and applied the concepts, symbols and metaphors by which people believe reality impacts their lives.

All people, by virtue of their being mortal, finite humans, experience the numinous sense of creaturehood. All people adopt symbols, myths or metaphors of some sort by which they seek to express and to understand the experience of the mysterium tremendum. All people, to some degree or another, accept some concepts and at least part of some overarching paradigm to give their lives meaning.

There seem to be at least three routes the peoples of earth follow in this quest for an understanding of reality. The first road is that taken by autonomous persons. When confronted by the numinous or the mysterium tremendum, these persons may call forth either out of their own archetypal unconscious or out of their cultural background, completely human symbols, metaphors, concepts and paradigms in an effort to explain the nameless mystery of their existence. They rely on images and concepts developed by the human psyche as it interacts with reality. These may be followers of positivistic science or of Marxism or of some highly sophisticated philosophic system.

A second route may be taken by those who, when confronted by the numinous, respond with a mixture of human, autonomously crafted metaphors, concepts and paradigms stimulated by the mysterium tremendum. It is apparent that Gautama's enlightenment, Confucious' moralizing and Lao Tzu's philosophizing give evidence of man's autonomous reason actively and creatively responding to the impact of natural reality upon them. They autonomously produced philosophies and perspectives which resulted from stimulation by the numinous.

Still a third route has been followed by those who, in response to the numinous experiences of life, have felt inspired by a higher being which they claimed actually communicated to them not only feelings of creatureliness but also words, symbols, metaphors, and concepts (propositions) which then were assembled into paradigms either by them or by their followers. Muhammed was one of these. Judaism and primitive Christianity also used words, metaphors, and concepts (propositions) which claimed divine authority with the words "Thus saith the Lord." The claims of Hebrew prophets, Christian apostles and Muhammed were that they had received laws, prophecies, messages and even divinely inspired words from God. Such claims make Islam and the Judeo-Christian religion discontinuous with most other religions because they attribute their symbols, metaphors, and concepts to divine inspiration whereas most religions and philosophies attribute their metaphors and concepts to human insights and accomplishments. Biblical religion also teaches a great discontinuity between a holy God and sinful humanity whereas most other religions, including Islam, see man as possessing autonomy and a continuity with ultimate reality so that man by his own devotion and works can rise to become one with the Holy One. The Bible is unique in that it alone describes man as totally dependent upon the sovereign Lord both for knowledge of the Holy and for union with Him. The Bible makes it clear that a unique Saviour who used symbols but who was Himself more than a symbol is God Incarnate bridging the gulf between the Infinite and humanity.

The classical theologians saw all people receiving some light from the general revelation God has given of Himself in the natural order. Special revelation through the historical Jesus Christ, however, was necessary for salvation or union with God. Yet general and special revelation were complementary and consistent one with another. Could it be that in a time when Christians travel freely across the world and understand more fully the teachings of other religions, they understand more clearly how God has shone His light through the multitudinous numinous experiences of people in other religions? Could it be that it becomes more apparent that God through all ages has been revealing both human creatureliness and the sovereignty of the ultimate as humans encounter the mysterium tremendum? Could it be that some persons through openness, obedience, and surrender to the light of general revelation have come very close to Christ, the second person of the Trinity, even though they know not His name? Though the symbols metaphors, concepts, and paradigms of most of the world's religions may be autonomous or semiautonomous expressions of numinous experiences, at their core they all highlight man's finitude and the ultimate's sovereignty.

Christians, believing in God's general revelation to all people, can discern the movement of the Triune God amongst all the peoples of earth. They see God approaching people dimly in the mysterium tremendum. They see Him revealing Himself as the Sovereign. They see Him revealing to people their finitude. At the same time they understand His yearning to complete His general revelation with a special revealing of His mercy and love in His Triunity.

Christians must come to the realization that the Triune God is at work in each of the billions of earth. He overshadows and underlies their lives and is at work in their cultures. He seeks to prepare them for an additional revelation of Himself in the Gospel. If, through a revitalized church, the peoples of earth could catch a clear vision of the Triune God as the universal mysterium tremendum, the named nameless, the universal way (Logos, Tao), they could find in Him the basis for a new cultural unity.

That does not suggest a new, syncretistic blending of various insights extracted from various religions. That would deny the heart of Christianity which is the particularity and uniqueness of Jesus Christ, His atonement, and His resurrection.

What it suggests is a model for culture which is holographic (multidimensional) rather than flat (two dimensional). Traditionally, the peoples of earth have thought in polar terms, with the ultimate and the world as the two contrasting poles. This has left culture with some difficult questions. How do the one and the many relate? How do intelligibility and materiality relate? The two dimensional view of reality is inadequate to resolve many issues of life.

A holographic view of reality, on the other hand, sees reality composed of the material, the mental, and the spiritual as multidimensional. Seen holographically, reality resembles a pyramid. The pyramid has three separate parts, the base (matter), the cap or peak (spirit) and the mid-section (the mental). Each part of the pyramid is multisided. Just as Pascal saw these three orders separated by abysses which cannot be bridged by natural or autonomous man, a holographic model of reality shows the material realm unable to provide power to subdue its primal impulses, the mental realm unable to provide satisfactory answers to the dilemmas of human existence and the spiritual realm alienated from the lower orders. The three orders of existence are separated and alienated from each other. Raw nature, by itself, cannot ascend into the mental realm. Neither can rationality by itself ascend into the realm of the spirit because it is paralyzed either by contradictions or egocentric predicaments. People who live for material power or riches alone are blinded by sensuality and are crushed by fragmentation and alienation. People who live for the intellect alone become frustrated by relativism, contradictions, and dead ends. Only when they are surrendered to the One who presides over all at the summit of reality do they find wholeness and meaning in existence. People standing at the base of the pyramid can see one or at most two of its sides. They have but a partial view of reality. Only when one sees from the peak of the pyramid can one see it as a whole.

When a person who has experienced the ultimate love and forgiveness of the Triune God sees reality from the apex (the realm of spiritual love), one imperfectly sees reality as a unified whole. People then can see all three sides and all three segments of the pyramid. When seen from the perspective of the divine Trinity (the spiritual order of divine love), the spiritual realm flows into the mental and material realms. In the light of God's spirit, the intellectual problems begin to find their resolution in God's revelation. In the light of God's love, the primal impulses of matter begin to find direction, harmony, order and intelligibility. It is the view from the pinnacle of the pyramid which can unify all things, can give meaning and harmony to all things and which can equip people to build a new world.

The apex of the pyramid represents the Triune God eternally made visible in Jesus Christ. The Christ event by which God came in the flesh into history is the culmination and fulfillment of all the mystical longings and experiences of humankind. It was uniquely historical and "einmaligkeit" in comparison with the timeless, transcendent and cyclical religions of the world. Lesslie Newbigin aptly has pointed out that many religions are non-historical. They are typified by the rotating wheel where all things change but where the center is timeless, unchanging and still. Not so, with the Triune God. Yes, all things change but He who is unchanging is involved in all things and particularly has shown His involvement by coming to earth at a specific time in a tiny land poised between east and west.

The model of a pyramid suggests that Biblical historical revelation (at the apex) unifies and gives meaning to all things including the non-historical impulses and thoughts scattered throughout the pyramid. It sifts the true from the false, the meaningful from the non-meaningful elements of human experience. It explains and synthesizes all things under the Triune God who by His spirit and by His Son works through the numinous (general revelation) to touch all people and through Scripture (special revelation) to touch the elect.

When people by encounters with the numinous or the mysterium tremendum approach the peak of reality, they perceive the sovereignty of someone or something. They may call it Brahman, Nirvana, heaven or the Tao, but they basically are aware of ultimate reality. A vision of the Triune God could enable them to understand that behind the mysterium tremendum they have encountered is God-Father, Son, Spirit waiting to give them a new revelation. Such a vision could clarify, purify, and reconstruct their symbols, metaphors, concepts and paradigms so that they could have a clearer understanding of the power of divine love to unify, to harmonize and to give meaning to all the orders of reality. Such a vision might result in Christians and non-Christians alike discarding some of their culturally shaped metaphors and replacing them with symbols and metaphors which more accurately reflect and interpret the ultimate who has revealed Himself first dimly as the numinous then more clearly as the Triune God.

The Triune God offers Himself to humanity not only for its salvation but also as the paradigm for all persons and cultures to follow. Jesus Christ, eternally God the Son, has given symbols, metaphors, and concepts which can become a paradigm for all people. He is sovereign, holy love who offers pardon and newness to all. He is infinitely free and just. The Trinity is perfect community and perfect righteousness. It shows true personhood. *If individuals and churches would enshrine the Triune God in their midst, societies could be influenced and changed and eventually a new world could be born.* Even though human sinfulness, arrogance, and pride make it unlikely that such a new world will be realized in time and space, it is a vision worth pursuing as we press into the future seeking more and more of Him and His reality. Understanding something of the Triune God is only a beginning. The fulfillment of the Christian's quest, indeed fulfillment for all mankind, begins but never ends with an exploration into the life of the Father, Son, and Holy Spirit. So we conclude this chapter with the hope that humanity will move forward into the numinous, into the mysterium tremendum, and ultimately into the Triune God who reaches outward toward every person and every culture. Knowledge of the Trinity is just the beginning of the great adventure into God and His reality.

NOTES

[1] cf. Van Til, Henry, *The Calvinistic Concept of Culture*, (Grand Rapids, Baker Book House, 1972). Dr. Van Til gives an excellent analysis of the cultural mandate as understood through the centuries.

[2] Quoted by Bahm, Archie, *Comparative Philosophy*, (Albuquerque, World Books, 1977), p.19.

[3] Hymn X.129, quoted in *A Source Book in Indian Philosophy*, ed. by S. Radhakrishnan and C. A. Moore, (Princeton, Princeton University Press, 1957).

[4] Chan, Wing-tsit. *A Source Book in Chinese Philosophy*, (Princeton, Princeton University Press, 1963), p.139.

[5] Otto, Rudolph. *The Idea of The Holy*, (London, Oxford University Press, 1957), p.10.

[6] Ibid., p.146.

[7] Ibid., p.177.

[8] Ibid., p.116.

[9] *The Bhagavad Gita*, translated by F. Edgerton, (Cambridge, Harvard University Press, 1972), pp.56–60,90.

[10] Quoted in *Great Asian Religions*, Fry, King, Swanger, Wolf, (Grand Rapids, Baker Book House, 1984), p.57.

[11] Ibid., p.73.

12 Fung, Yu Lan, *A Short History of Chinese Philosophy* ed. by D. Bodde, (New York, The Free Press-MacMillan, 1948), p.47.

13 Fung, Yu Lan, *A History of Chinese Philosophy,* translated by D. Bodde, (Princeton, Princeton University Press, 1983), p.57.

14 Ibid., p.58.

15 Ibid., p.58.

16 Ibid., p.58.

17 Ibid., p.97.

18 Ibid., p.177.

19 Ibid., p.178.

20 Ibid., p.178.

21 Ibid., p.384, *The Book of Changes* (I Ching), which deals with yin and yang, profoundly influenced Lao-Tzu and Chuang-Tzu, who elaborated further on yin and yang.

22 Ibid., p.179.

23 Ibid., p.190.

24 Langer, Suzanne K., *Philosophy in a New Key*, (New York, a Mentor Book New American Library, 1955), p.33.

25 McFague, Sallie, *Metaphorical Theology*, (Philadelphia, Fortress Press, 1982), p.35. McFague says a metaphor "finds the vein of similarity in the midst of dissimilars." A symbol "rests on similarity already present and assumed." p.17. She does not, however, acknowledge that symbol is more appropriate to revelation than metaphor.

26 Ibid., p.42.

Epilogue and Beginning

Grander than an artist painting a masterpiece, more wondrous than a sculptor shaping a fine statue, the Triune God has created a many-splendored universe which He is fashioning according to His purposes. He works with nature, with human society, and with individual lives, by both natural and special graces. In the process, the Divine artist has left brushstrokes in nature and footprints in human history which indicate the direction His purposes are moving.

Some of His people, however, confronted with a myriad of social, political, economic decisions, become confused. They believe they should follow the purposes of the Triune God, yet they don't know how they apply to specific situations. Many Christians are seeking an understanding of His will as it applies to society. Can the Trinity provide light to assist people to know and to do His will in the rough and tumble of practical, everyday life? Can finite people grasp the will of the transcendent Lord?

The Triune God has given Sacred Scripture to teach and to guide humanity. It is a truism, though, that almost anything can be proved by Scripture. For example, as God's people wrestle with difficult ethical questions, Biblical texts may be invoked both by those who are pro and by those who are con. People become perplexed when they hear some clergy cite texts which seem to suggest a redistributive, planned society while they hear other clergy quote texts which seem to advocate a free market society. Isolated Biblical passages taken out of context and used to bolster partisan convictions only add to confusion in a morally bewildered world.

Yet, there are important strands of Biblical thought pervading

Scripture. They can serve as middle axioms to mediate guidance from the transcendent Trinity to people confronted by confusing ethical situations. Those major themes running throughout Scripture deal with (1) God's relation to man/creation and (2) man's/creation's relation to God. Each of these fundamental themes is displayed in a host of passages scattered throughout the Bible. Each grows out of Biblical teachings about the nature of the Triune God.

When a person's heart and mind become saturated with these themes and with the Biblical perspective, he becomes a mediating link between the transcendent Lord and the tangled web of human affairs. The teaching which comes to dominate his heart and mind has many facets. Central to them are the two great themes from which flow ancillary principles which touch upon all areas of human life.

The two major themes which undergird all of Scripture are the relation of the sovereign God to creation (man) and the relation of creation (man) to God. Put another way, the *first* is: God's relation to creation as its Sovereign. A corollary to God's sovereignty is His wholeness, unity, and powerful love as He creates and recreates all things. The *second* is a fallen creation's relation to God as it is recreated and recreates all things into the wholeness, unity and love of God.

Since God is the sovereign Lord and gives existence to all things by His undergirding love and power, all things root in and are one in Him. His sovereign love and power sustain all things, but if He withdrew His presence for an instant from an amoeba or a giant star, either would cease to exist. Though all things depend on God, some parts of creation (i.e. humanity) have tried to become completely independent of Him. God is confronted by a Promethean world in rebellion, a world which His Son came to redeem and to reconcile to Himself. Through Jesus' death and resurrection, God has been offering to humankind a return to His wholeness, unity, and love. Reconciled men and women have been called to serve and to glorify God by being His instruments reconciling the world to Him. (2 Cor. 5:17–20) Reconciliation can restore and actualize both the sovereignty of God and the wholeness of reality in Him. Reconciliation is God's work (Col. 1:19,20), but Christ's men and women are privileged to participate in it.

If the notion of the sovereignty of God and the wholeness and unity of reality in His love is a valid middle axiom, how does it guide God's people in their decision making? First, it must be understood that the wholeness of reality in God carries with it an awareness of reality's dependence upon the sovereign God and of the interrelatedness and unity of all the facets of reality in Him. God is one, therefore, all the facets of reality, being upheld by Him, are dependent upon Him and interrelated in Him. Alienated from Him, any portion of reality becomes lost, adrift in an abyss of nothingness.

The interrelatedness of all parts of reality reflects something of the interrelatedness, dimensionality, perichoresis, community, and unity of the three persons in the Godhead. The unity and relatedness of all things was conceived by the Father, made possible by the Son, and actualized by the Holy Spirit. Each part of reality has its source in God. Each is complementary to the others. Each is a part of the whole and, in some way, fits into the whole scheme of things. Each was intended to bring glory to God. Everything in the cosmos was and will be part of a "good" creation.

When a Christian person, then, has a decision to make, he or she must seek to view the situation as part of the totality of things. He must consider its context, which is God's sovereign rule. He must view the situation in the light of God's purpose to unify all things in His love. He must make his decision for or against a course of action upon the basis of whether or not it will bring the people and things involved closer to union with God, closer to a oneness and harmony with the created order, and closer to a free, loving community which mirrors that of the Triune community. The wholeness and interrelatedness of reality in the sovereign Triune God thus becomes the context and an important touch-stone for ethical decision-making.

Intimately related to that grand, Scriptural theme (God's relation to man) is the reconciliation of all things into the wholeness of God's reality. (Man's relation to God) That reconciliation is to be brought about by (a) the humanization of God and (b) the divinization of humanity. Since humanity first sought its independence from God, reality has been rifted by a great gulf of alienation between God and His creation. To bridge the chasm, God the Spirit approaches people through the mysterium tremendum and God the incarnate Son has sought and still seeks to reconcile a lost world. The humanization of God reached its climax when Jesus agonized on a cross outside Jerusalem. Jesus was God being "tempted in all points like as we yet without sin." (Heb. 4:15) Jesus wept, hungered, suffered, and died. He was truly man as well as truly God.

God in human form expressed the basic character of the whole Triune God. He demonstrated the reconciling, self-giving love which binds the three into one divine community. He displayed their freedom, equality and justice. As people gazed upon Him, they saw the others in the Godhead through Him. (i.e. "He that hath seen me hath seen the Father." John 14:9)

In a world burdened with slavery, He made visible the freedom of God which was to be let loose in human society. ("And the Truth shall make you free" John 8:32) In a world where human life was devalued, He loved each person sacrificially and lifted human worth to the heights. In a world where most people merely were impersonally associated, He established His church as a beachhead of that loving, reconciling community which reflects the ultimate community in the Triune God. Freedom, equality, and the justice of self-giving love in community were established as foundational values in western culture, at least in part, through His incarnational humanization.

The full orbed experience of freedom which arose from people's identification with the God of infinite freedom stimulated a devotion to liberty across the centuries of western history. Though many lesser freedoms born of identifications with finite realities also have arisen, they have but imitated the most sublime of freedoms. The coming of the infinitely free One released a wave of freedom into world culture.

In contemporary ethical decision making, Christians need to

give priority to that which will enable people to experience and to live by the highest freedom. This suggests that Christians need to discriminate among the various freedoms being proposed today. Does the freedom proposed arise from an identification with the infinitely free God or from some earthly identification? It must be recognized that many contemporary movements are based on pseudo freedoms which could backfire destroying larger freedoms. Therefore, Christians must select carefully the freedom movements they support.

Some of today's freedom movements are based on human pride. Others arise from greed or a love of power or envy. Ultimately, they will self-destruct as they clash with other earth-bound claims to freedom. Only freedom based on an identification with the God who wills that all should share in His freedom has the capacity to embrace and to reconcile all people, classes and races. The freedom which comes from God is counterpoised with an awareness that God's reconciling love can dissolve the base, worldly motives and actions which inhibit true freedom.

God's humanization, both in the Incarnation and in His living in and through believers, also has made visible to the world the just, reconciling, selfgiving, sacrificial love of the Triune God. Christ in agony on the cross and believers giving themselves for their fellow humans have let loose a wave of compassion and community which has affected culture deeply. Yet, that love is vastly different from the sentimental, permissive love of 20th century western society. The Father in love gave His Son to die a shameful death. Christ in love drove money changers from His Father's temple and pronounced judgment on whited sepulchers. God's love at times may be sharp, prodding, and painful. Self-giving love does not ponder the effect of an action upon the subject's own ego. It considers only what is best for the object of love even though that may mean chastening.

The humanization of the Triune God, then, suggests that freedom and reconciling, self-giving love in community are the primary criteria to be considered in ethical decision making. What will enhance the highest freedom under God of people in this or that situation? What decision will be most in accord with God's self-giving love, and what action will move persons in the situation toward demonstrating a just reconciliation toward others? What action will produce a reconciled community of free persons resembling the community of love in the Triune God?

The humanization of God and the divinization of man both are necessary ingredients in the reconciliation of reality with God. Humanization brings God into union with people. Divinization brings people into union with God. Each is peculiarly Trinitarian. In the humanization of God, it is the Father in whose mind humanity existed before it was created. The Father sent the Son to make reconciliation and divine humanization possible. It is the Son who embodies and reveals true humanity. It is the Holy Spirit who achieves the humanization of God in believers. At the same time, it is the Holy Spirit who, by applying the work of Jesus Christ to individual hearts, enables man to participate in the life of God. It is the Son who gathers to Himself all believers and presents them as one with Himself to the Father.

The divinization of man is the lifting of humanity into the realm of divine life. It results from the reconciling union of persons with God. As Christ, by the Spirit, is formed in human lives, humanity becomes divinely autonomous. The new divinized humanity exhibits a joyous freedom in God. It demonstrates that justice is actualized in obedience to God's holy will. The new humanity expresses the just, self-giving love of the Triune God. It becomes a prototype of eternal life in God's presence. It enables Christians to become truly autonomous and self-de-terminative in God and frees them from the oppressive, heteronomous forces in life.

This divinization of humanity should be a significant factor in the decision making of Christians even as the humanization of God ought to be. Both are necessary to achieve the reconciliation which is a major theme of the Bible. As believers act in culture, they constantly should be considering ways to stimulate reconciliation of persons with God and with each other as well as to stimulate their growth in free, loving community. They ought to be creating and recreating, reconciling, new institutions and services which will bring about true community and will enable persons to grow in faith, in freedom, in self-giving love, and in that justice by which people freely will act in accord with His life and will become more and more like Jesus.

This means that creative new forms of the church may be needed. People's needs will not be satisfied with praying and paying or with hearing sermons which are rehashes of the *New York Times* and *Time* magazine. If divinization is to become a reality, the church must really become the Body of Christ which feeds on the Word of God, which moves out into society, banners unfurled, to witness and to serve as Christ did. If a revitalized church emerges, other institutions in society could be pointed toward the values which flow from the Triune God and could be renewed. *As a reborn church expresses the sovereignty of God, the wholeness and unity of all in Him, the humanization of the Triune God, and the divinization of humankind*, large portions of society could be transformed and the beginnings of a new, just world community could be born.

We began this study wondering whether or not a new vision of the Triune God could inspire a new social order. We conclude unable to demonstrate that a Trinitarian perspective is changing things today. Yet, those who know the Triune God have a hope born of faith. That hope is buttressed by the history of the Christian movement which, at times, has transformed people into gloriously free, just human beings and has changed human society. God's people have faith that with God all things are possible. So they march on seeking to enthrone the Triune God in the affairs of this world. So may "the kingdoms of this world become the kingdoms of our God and of His Christ." Alleluia.

Bibliography

Aquinas, Thomas. *Basic Writings*. Edited by Anton Pegis. 2 vol. New York: Random House, 1945.
Aristotle. *The Basic Works of Aristotle*. Edited by Richard McKeon. New York: Random House, 1941.
Augustine. *The City of God*. New York: Image Books, 1958.
———. *The Fathers of the Church, The Trinity*. Vol. 45. Washington, D.C.: The Catholic University Press, 1981.
Bahm, Archie. *Comparative Philosophy*. Albuquerque: World Books, 1977.
Barnett, Lincoln. *The Universe and Dr. Einstein*. New York: Bantam Books, 1980.
Barth, Karl. *The Doctrine of the Word of God*. Vol. 1. Edinburgh: T. and T. Clark, 1949
Bloesch, Donald G. *The Battle for the Trinity*. Ann Arbor: Servant Publications, 1985.
Bracken, Joseph A. *The Triune Symbol*. Lanham, MD: University Press of America, 1985.
Brunner, Emil. *The Divine Imperative*. Philadelphia: Westminster Press, 1947.
———. *The Christian Doctrine of Creation and Redemption*. Philadelphia: Westminster Press, 1952.
Bultmann, R. *Theology of the New Testament*. 2 vol. New York: Scribner's, 1951, 1955.
Butterfield, Herbert. *The Origins of Modern Science*. London: G. Bell and Sons, 1957.
Cailliet, Emile. *The Christian Approach to Culture*. Nashville: Abingdon-Cokesbury, 1953.
Calvin, John. *Institutes of the Christian Religion*. 2 vol. Philadelphia: Westminster Press, 1960.
Chan, Wing-Tsit. *A Source Book in Chinese Philosophy*. Princeton: Princeton University Press, 1963.
Chardin, Teilhard de. *The Phenomenon of Man*. New York: Harpers, 1959.
Cochrane, Charles. *Christianity and Classical Culture*. New York: Oxford University Press, 1944.
Conant, James B. *On Understanding Science*. New York: Mentor Books, 1951.

―――. *Modern Science and Modern Man.* New York: Doubleday, 1953.
Cornford, F.M. *Before and After Socrates.* New York: Cambridge University Press, 1960.
Dampier, William C. *A Shorter History of Science.* New York: Meridian Books, 1957.
D'Arcy, M.C. et.al. *Thomas Aquinas.* Maryland: Newman Bookshop, 1944.
―――. *St. Augustine.* New York: Meridian Books, 1957.
Dewart, Leslie. *The Future of Belief.* New York: Herder and Herder, 1966.
Dupre, Louis. *The Common Life.* New York: Crossroad, 1984.
Eckhardt, Meister. *Breakthrough.* New York: Image Books, 1980.
Edgerton, F. *The Bhagavad Gita.* Cambridge: Harvard University Press, 1972.
Einstein, A., and Infeld, L. *The Evolution of Physics.* New York: Simon and Schuster, 1938.
Eliot, T.S. *Christianity and Culture.* New York: Harcourt, Brace, Janovich, 1968.
Fung, Yu Lan. *A Short History of Chinese Philosophy.* Edited by D. Bodde. New York: Free Press, 1948.
Fry, C. George; King, J.R.; Swanger, E.R.; and Wolf, H.C. *Great Asian Religions.* Grand Rapids: Baker Book House, 1984.
Fortman, Edmund J. *The Triune God.* Grand Rapids: Baker Book House, 1972.
Gilkey, Langdon. *Society and the Sacred.* New York: Crossroad, 1981.
Hegel, G.W.F. *Encyclopedia of Philosophy.* New York: Philosophical Library, 1959.
Heim, Karl. *Christian Faith and Natural Science.* New York: Harpers, 1953.
Hodgson, Leonard. *The Doctrine of the Trinity.* London: Nisbet, 1946.
Jenson, Robert W. *The Triune Identity.* Philadelphia: Fortress Press, 1982.
Jungel, Eberhard. *The Doctrine of the Trinity.* Grand Rapids: Eerdmans, 1976.
Kuhn, Thomas S. *The Structure of Scientific Revolutions.* Chicago: University of Chicago, 1970.
Langer, Suzanne K. *Philosophy in a New Key.* New York: Mentor Books, 1955.
Leith, John H. ed. *Creeds of the Churches.* New York: Doubleday, 1963.
Lewis, C.S. *The Abolition of Man.* New York: MacMillan, 1975.
Mackintosh, Hugh R. *Types of Modern Theology.* London: Nisbet, 1947.
MacKenzie, Charles. *Pascal's Anguish and Joy.* New York: Philosophical Library, 1973.
McFague, Sallie. *Metaphorical Theology.* Philadelphia: Fortress Press, 1982.
Migliore, Daniel. *Called to Freedom.* Philadelphia: Westminster Press, 1980.
―――. "The Trinity and Human Liberty." *Theology Today.* (January, 1980).
Miller, Haskell M. *A Christian Critique of Culture.* Nashville: Abingdon, 1965.
Moltmann, Jurgen. *The Trinity and the Kingdom.* San Francisco: Harper and Row, 1981.